POSITIVELY OBEDIENT

OBEDIENT

Good Manners For The Family Dog

Barbara S. Handler

illustrations by Mary Alice Smiley

1987
Alpine Publications, Inc.

Library of Congress Cataloging in Publication Data

Handler, Barbara S.
  Positively obedient.

  Bibliography: p.
  Includes index.
  1. Dogs—Training. I. Title.
SF431.H24   1987   636.7 '088   86-32134
ISBN 0-931866-28-6

International Standard Book No. 0-931866-28-6
Library of Congress Catalog Card No. 86-32134

First edition—1987
Printed in the United States of America.

To my canine friends
who have enriched my life
and taught me much about love and loyalty.

Contents

Foreword

During the many years I have been involved with dog obedience as a trainer and an obedience judge, I have seen important and positive changes take place in our understanding of dog behavior and how we can produce the kind of pet that is an asset in our lives, not a liability. There have been some terrific books written about dogs and positive methods of training, but all of these books are either technical volumes geared to an audience of behavioral scientists, or they are aimed at people who want to compete in formal obedience trials with their dogs. They cover training exercises which, in my experience, are not useful to the pet owner. They are large, expensive volumes.

This book was written for you, the average dog owner, who wants your dog to enhance your lifestyle, not be a constant irritant. I will not try to overwhelm you with difficult psychological concepts, or to give you information that is not immediately useful. I will give you the names of a number of other books where such information is available. I will try to make this new knowledge of animal behavior available to you in a form which you can use to bring your dog under control and establish a positive relationship with your family pet. This book is not intended to be absolutely comprehensive; rather it is meant to focus on positive methods of training your dog and building a better relationship between the two of you. It is not a manual for the person who wants to exhibit his or her dog in formal obedience competitions. There are no magic methods in this book, no instant secrets for perfect obedience. We are beginning an ongoing process which can take you to whatever level you want to reach with your dog, from basic control to advanced training, to any number of avenues in which you and your pet can enhance each other's lives.

This book will not address in detail how to handle problems such as jumping up, housesoiling, or chewing because I believe that many behavioral problems will disappear once you and your dog learn the obedience exercises outlined herein. Once you can set clear limits for your dog and enforce them appropriately, behavior problems often are eliminated by this simple change in your relationship. For example, a dog that jumps on people can be told to sit and stay, and voila! no more problem. If you continue to experience intolerable problems with your dog after you have both mastered the obedience exercises, you may want to seek professional help. Some veterinarians have expertise in this area, but many vets never receive training in canine behavior. Your vet may refer you to an animal behaviorist, or you may be able to find a listing for a behaviorist in the phone book. These are people who have had specialized training in canine and feline behavior problems. If you do consult one of these behaviorists, ask questions about his or her background and training. A competent behaviorist will generally have had both academic training and hands-on experience in working with problem animals.

I will present some concepts in *Positively Obedient* which are not addressed in many obedience books geared for the general public. I strongly urge you to read the entire book before starting any actual work with your dog. In this way, you will have a complete picture of what you want to accomplish and be aware of possible training obstacles before you ever pick up the leash. You will be more confident and more competent when you are ready to begin communication with your pet in the actual training process.

Acknowledgements

A lot of people helped make this book possible. I'd like to single out a few here for special thanks. To the people and the dogs who posed for the pictures, thanks for your patience and willingness to do it again and again until the photographer could get herself in gear. All of the people and dogs in the pictures are identified on page 173. My gratitude to my efficient and sharp-eyed friend and secretary, Juanita Westcott, for deciphering my scratchings and producing readable copy. Special thanks to the folks who read the manuscript—Sandra Burns, Mary Covell, Charles and Shirley O'Brien, Mary Belle Reusch, Julie Yamane and my technical adviser and trusted veterinarian, John Mulnix—I appreciate your many helpful comments and suggestions. Finally, my deepest thanks to all of my students, both human and canine, who have enabled me to experiment, learn and grow over the years as teacher and trainer, and often friend.

Why Train
Your Dog?

A trained dog is a better pet—that is the bottom line. An untrained dog is a nuisance to its family and frequently to the community. Dogs that have received the kind of training outlined in this book rarely end their days being euthanized (put to sleep) at the local animal shelter. A trained dog can go places and do things an untrained dog cannot. A small untrained dog is usually obnoxious, barking uncontrollably, doing minor damage in the home, harassing people and generally making itself unwelcome. A large untrained dog can be a dangerous and costly liability, causing extensive property damage and hurting people. The saddest untrained dog is the one who has slipped his collar, bolted out the door, or simply taken advantage of being allowed to run loose, and is gone. Anyone who has lost a beloved dog knows the heartbreak felt by the entire family, especially when the dog's fate remains unknown for any period of time.

Dogs (and other pets) are becoming less and less welcome in many areas. Landlords and motel owners have had their fill of complaints about continuous barking, not to mention the property damage caused by uncontrolled dogs on their premises. Parks and recreation departments are closing their grounds to these canine delinquents who are allowed to bowl over or attack children, leap into the middle of family picnics, or leave unaesthetic and unhealthy messes in places people want to walk or sit.

None of this is the fault of any dog. It is the ignorant, uncaring or irresponsible owners who thoughtlessly permit these behaviors who force everyone else to be burdened with anti-dog restrictions. In this age of the instant lawsuit, I wonder about the intelligence of an owner who allows his or her dog to run loose, fouling property and terrorizing passers-by. I would think that these people would at least worry about their liability costs in the event of a dog bite, not to mention the potential for causing someone pain and disfigurement.

Obedience training has some very positive aspects. It allows us to try to comprehend the needs of a creature whose point of view is very different from our own. Our dogs provide us with an ongoing link with the natural world, away from buttons to be pushed and switches to be flipped. What is more, when training is done using the methods outlined in this book, it is FUN for both parties involved. Finally, I believe we owe it to our dogs to set reasonable and consistent limits, as we owe it to our children. Dogs need to understand the rules of the house, so that they can go on about their daily business without constantly having to test to see if a certain behavior is permitted on Tuesday when it was forbidden on Monday. Testing limits takes a great deal of energy and creates frustration for both pet and human.

Fig. 1-1. A trained dog becomes a special friend able to share many experiences with you.

In addition to saving wear and tear on the owner, obedience training is basic to other dog-related activities. Many people enjoy teaching their dogs tricks for fun and amusement (and to show off for the neighbors). Basic obedience is a prerequisite for most tricks. Hunters obedience train their dogs and call it "yard manners," so the dog will be under control in the field. As one hunter commented, "It is a lot more fun to hunt with a dog that brings the bird back to you than one that takes it under the truck and eats it."

As behavioral scientists explore the mutual benefits of the human-animal companion bond they are formalizing what we pet lovers have known for years: that our animal companions are far more than fuzzy footwarmers. They can soothe and comfort and even help restore our mental and physical health. The whole area of "pet-facilitated therapy" is bringing dogs and other animals into hospitals, nursing homes, mental health treatment facilities, and other institutions. Clearly, basic obedience is important for a dog in such surroundings.

MORE APPLICATIONS FOR TRAINING

Like many other innocents who wander into local obedience classes to make Rover mind, I somehow found myself, several months later, standing in the middle of an American Kennel Club (AKC) obedience trial, dog in hand and feeling bewildered. Little did I know that the pattern for my weekends for many years to come was being set. In AKC (or United Kennel Club [UKC], a competing and less extensive organization) obedience trials, owners of purebred registered dogs perform a standard set of exercises and are judged for correct execution of each exercise, as well as accuracy and attitude. It is an artificial competition which provides a test of some facets of a dog's training. Obedience is a sport in which anyone with a purebred registered dog may compete, and you are likely to see older people, children, disabled people and people from all types of occupations coming together for the competition and the camaraderie week after week. Mixed-breed dogs and non-registerable purebreds can compete at informal competitions known as "matches" or "fun matches" and can earn titles as well. If you find that you and your dog are enjoying the very basic exercises outlined in this book, and would like to investigate this phase of training, refer to the bibliography. Remember, this book is not designed to prepare you and your dog for such competition. Also, see the section on Training in a Class (p.50).

If you own a registered purebred dog which is a good specimen of its breed, you may want to exhibit in AKC conformation shows, in which your dog may, if he is of good enough quality, earn enough points to become a champion. In order to compete in these shows, the dog must be trained to walk calmly on a leash and then stand still while a stranger (the judge) examines its body.

For those whose interests are a bit more esoteric, there are herding trials in which the various breeds used for controlling livestock are tested. The control and communication between dog and master at these trials will leave you open-mouthed. People who own Newfoundlands and other water-oriented breeds attend water tests. There is growing interest in terrier trials which test the natural anti-vermin instinct of many of the terrier breeds. Sighthounds (Afghan Hounds, Wolfhounds, Greyhounds, Whippets) compete in lure coursing races for fun and titles. The AKC and other organizations also sponsor structured field trials for various types of hunting activities. All of these activities allow you to explore your dog's natural instincts to see if he can still do the job for which his ancestors were originally bred, and all require some degree of obedience training.

There is one additional dog-centered activity I must mention. A growing number of people who own large guard dogs (German Shepherd Dogs, Dobermans, Rottweilers) participate in competitions in which dogs perform obedience exercises, follow scent trails and engage in what is euphemistically called "protection work" (read: biting people who are wearing protective clothing and pretending to be criminals). This combination of activities is known as "schutzhund" and is based on similar competitions traditional in Europe. I am not in favor of teaching pet dogs to bite people under any circumstances. I have carefully observed a number of schutzhund trials. My observations have consistently been that both dog and owner focus on the "protection" phase with enthusiasm, but many of the dogs I have observed have had only minimal obedience training and are not, in fact, under their owners' control. The selection of dogs to participate in this "sport" is frequently made with no understanding of dog behavior and with total disregard for the temperament of the dogs involved. People with shy dogs are told that teaching the dog "protection" will "bring the dog out" by increasing its self-confidence (and possibly bring the owner into a courtroom with a lawsuit). The training is often done irresponsibly and generally very harshly. I am certain there are responsible trainers involved in schutzhund who do understand that this activity is inappropriate for many people and many dogs. Unfortunately, responsible trainers appear to be in the minority. Dog owners should consider at length the risks to themselves and those with whom their dog comes in contact before involving themselves in the "sport" of schutzhund.

Similarly, any type of attack or guard training for a pet dog represents a serious potential risk for a pet owner. It is my firm belief that there is a place for attack-trained dogs, and it is not in the average person's back yard. The place for a trained guard dog is in the hands of a skilled and experienced professional in the military, the police, or other similar organization. Training, handling and maintaining such a dog requires judgment, skill, physical stamina, and the clear understanding that an animal processed to be used as a weapon (of either offense or defense) is a source of possible extreme danger as long as the animal lives. If you are absolutely certain you must have a guard dog, I advise you to buy a trained dog from a reputable professional rather than teach the family Poodle to attack on command. If I were going to buy a trained dog, I would only deal with a professional who had on-the-job experience in the military or with a law enforcement agency. Such a trainer would have had to depend on his or her dog in potentially life-threatening situations and therefore would understand the importance of being able to rely on the dog. Anyone can teach a dog to growl and bite. Only an experienced professional can judge if a dog has an appropriate temperament for guard dog training and can teach the dog when to show aggression and when to stop. Having said all of this, I still advise you to steer clear of any form of attack training for any dog you own.

2

Understanding Your
Dog's Learning
Process

I n spite of what loving and indulgent pet owners believe, dogs are not small people in furry suits; they are animals. Their behavior has some things in common with human behavior, but we must be careful in making generalized assumptions from one species to the other. I believe that dogs are capable of simple reasoning. Dog guides for the blind must make decisions which reflect this ability to reason. They learn that under some conditions approaching vehicles are safe, and under other conditions they are not. These are judgment calls, based on a certain amount of training and conditioning. An experienced herding dog shows evidence of reasoning ability, again enhanced by training and instinct. As is true with people, some dogs are better at thinking and reasoning than others, and all dogs must be encouraged to learn to think in order to get better at it. While some experts will disagree with me as to whether dogs reason, there can be no question that dogs feel; that they experience emotions which appear equivalent to our own emotions. It does not take an expert to know when a dog is happy, anxious, or frightened. A bit more skilled observation can reveal when a dog feels depressed, silly, bored or playful.

Training—teaching a previously unknown behavior—is to some extent stressful for all dogs. The methods you will learn in this book will be geared to minimize stress and anxiety for both you and the dog. Behavior is shaped (changed or patterned) by association. For example, a dog is gently placed in the sit position and simultaneously hears the word, "Sit." He is praised and/or given a food reward. Eventually, the dog begins to form the association between the word ("Sit"), the action (being placed in a sit) and the reward (praise or food). How many repetitions are needed before the dog makes the association and sits by himself when he hears the word "Sit" depends on a number of factors. These factors include: the complexity of the behavior (how many actions are involved), the dog's basic intelligence, past learning experience (dogs learn how to learn and can improve as more new things are taught), the trainer's attitude and degree of patience, how pleasurable the dog finds the behavior, and the amount of natural instinct involved with the behavior. Instinct is most evident in those behaviors for which certain breeds have been carefully bred for many generations. That is, it is generally much easier to teach a Border Collie to herd sheep than it is to teach the same skill to a Greyhound. Similarly, a Labrador Retriever will learn to fetch birds more quickly than a Fox Terrier.

Obedience training then involves a system of forming associations in the dog's mind between certain words or gestures made by the trainer and certain actions the trainer wants the dog to take. Most training is done with a combination of rewards and punishments (corrections) which are given to the dog when he responds or fails to respond to a word or gesture from the trainer. However, the methods you will learn in this book rely much more heavily on reward than punishment.

Fig. 2-1. Anybody can tell when a dog is happy....

If you were to keep a chart of the rate at which your dog learned a particular behavior it would not proceed upward in a straight line. Dogs learn in spurts; frequently reaching plateaus on which they seem to get stuck for days, learning nothing. As more complex behaviors are introduced, the learning process occasionally goes into reverse. Something the dog did perfectly on Monday will totally confuse him on Wednesday. With a few days or weeks of additional training, he will again be able to perform the behavior. This is normal learning behavior and most experienced trainers will not enter a dog in an obedience trial until the dog has "backslid" and recovered on all of the exercises he will be required to perform.

Dogs can begin to be taught desired behaviors as early as six weeks of age. Puppies can learn a wide variety of obedience exercises, but their attention spans are remarkably short. Any training done with a puppy should be limited to very short sessions. See page 10 for more on puppy training. When I am teaching formal obedience exercises for competition, I prefer to wait until the dog is old enough to have developed the capacity to concentrate (generally between nine and fourteen months). Furthermore, while puppies are ready to learn at an early age, they have a great deal of emotional development to go through. It is normal for a puppy suddenly to become fearful, rebellious, or aggressive at different times during his first year with no apparent cause. These mood swings need to be noticed and considered during training.

Fig. 2-2. ...Or sad.

While it is always risky to make generalizations because of the tremendous variety within each breed, it is frequently true that different breeds (or mixes of those breeds) learn at different rates. I suspect this has more to do with willingness to please than it does with native intelligence.

Technically speaking, the dogs that learn obedience exercises fastest are the most trainable, not necessarily the smartest. In fact, obedience trial exhibitors whose dogs must be drilled for accuracy and precision often prefer a dog that is not overly bright but very willing. Bright dogs tend to get bored easily and invent new variations on the required exercises, much to their owners' dismay. Not surprisingly, the most trainable breeds are generally those bred to work closely with man. These include the retrievers, various sheep and cattle herding dogs, and the companion breeds, such as the Poodle and some of the toy breeds. Conversely, breeds that were bred to work independently tend to be less amenable to obedience work. These include many of the hound breeds, the terriers, and some of the Northern breeds (Huskies, Malamutes, Chows). This does not, of course, mean that all German Shepherd Dogs are easy to train or that all Dachshunds are difficult. (See Chapter 9 for more details about how different breeds of dogs learn.)

THE BEST AGE FOR TRAINING

How much and how effectively you can teach a puppy depends on you and the puppy. While all dog training requires patience, training puppies requires infinite patience. As previously stated, a puppy will begin learning as early as six weeks. It would be logical to teach it to behave the way you want from the outset as it is harder to eliminate an undesirable behavior the puppy has learned on its own than to build the desired behavior in the first place. However, your expectations must be realistic and you must keep in mind the puppy's limited attention span and your own degree of patience. With large dogs, it is essential that training begin while you can physically manipulate the puppy. If you are successful, your dog will never suspect he is stronger than you are.

Puppy training should be as positive as possible until the dog is about five to six months old, with little or no correction of any kind. A puppy is not ready for correction until he has matured mentally and emotionally. Training should build and enhance the puppy's self confidence, not threaten it. All the methods described in this book for teaching the exercises can be applied to puppies. They should only be done for a few minutes at a time, and should be done in a quiet place with minimal distraction. Work on only one behavior at a time. Be sure to build play into your training sessions.

What things should a puppy know? By the age of six months, I expect (but don't always get what I expect) my puppy to be housebroken, to stay off the furniture, to put his mouth only on his own toys and not on my carpets or furniture or me, to accept the dog crate, (see p. 117) to walk on a leash without acting like a bucking horse or insisting on going a different direction than the one I am going, to ride in a car (usually confined to a dog crate), to stand or lie still for grooming, to come when he is called in an enclosed area (house, yard or training building), to permit any part of his body to be handled, and to have a basic understanding of the words "sit" and "down." Since my dogs are also show dogs, they learn to tolerate crowds and the presence of numerous other dogs, as well. I also teach my puppies to play retrieving games, but if a pup is not interested I do not push the issue. That is a lot to learn in a few short months. During that time, I must remain aware of physical changes such as teething that affect my puppy, as well as natural stages of emotional development, including a shy stage and an independent (No, I *won't*) stage.

You must be reasonable in your expectations of how much and how fast your puppy can learn. If you push too hard, the puppy will show increasing signs of stress. Depending on the puppy's individual temperament, he may show anxiety by avoiding you or by reverting to house soiling. He may become hyper at training time or put on the brakes and become stubborn. Back off and wait a few days; then start again, being careful to work on only one behavior at a time, and to avoid any correction or punishment. If the pup makes a mistake, help him do the behavior right and praise and reward him. If you have a young puppy, or if you are planning to acquire one, I strongly urge you to read the book *How to Raise a Puppy You Can Live With* by Rutherford and Neil, which is the best reference I know on puppy-rearing and will serve as a good companion piece to this book.

When is a dog too old to train? Never! I have had some elderly canines enrolled in my obedience classes and they have generally done well. Occasionally there are dominance issues to be settled, (see p. 19) and sometimes the seniors can't sit or lie down quite as quickly as the young whipper-snappers, but the older dogs are capable of sustained attention and are usually calmly accepting of new behaviors.

3

Two
Approaches
to Dog Training

There are two basic ways to train a dog. Traditionally, dogs have been trained through *pain avoidance*. With this method, the dog is corrected or punished, usually with the fast closing of the choke chain on his throat, until he performs the desired behavior. For example, to teach a dog to sit using pain avoidance, the dog is given the command, "Sit." At the same time, the trainer jerks the collar sharply upwards on the dog's neck and pushes downward or slaps the dog on the rump. As the dog sits, the pain of the collar stops and the dog is usually praised ("Good dog"). After a certain number of repetitions, the rump push is eliminated and the dog learns to sit when he hears the command in order to avoid the pain of the collar pull.

The other method for teaching a behavior is the *inducive* or *positive reward* method. In this method, the dog is gently physically manipulated into the desired position as he is given a corresponding command or *cue word*. Then he is rewarded. The dog begins to make a positive association between the cue word, the physical positioning, and the reward (either food or praise or both). To teach the sit, the dog is gently positioned in a sit as he hears the cue word, "Sit." He is held in that position for a few seconds and then rewarded. The dog cannot make a mistake because he is physically prevented from doing so. Alternatively, a piece of food may be held above the dog's head and moved backwards, in the direction of his tail. The cue word is spoken. As the dog's nose comes up to smell the food, his rear end naturally drops to the ground (or he will fall over) and he assumes the sit position. He is given the food and praised.

What are the benefits and drawbacks of pain avoidance vs. inducive methods? Pain avoidance generally gets faster results than positive reward training. Consider which would be more effective: your boss offers you a raise if you will do certain additional duties, or your boss tells you to do certain things or be fired. You are likely to respond more promptly to the second alternative, which is a form of pain avoidance, but your anxiety level is also likely to skyrocket. In some cases, being pushed too hard (threatened with being fired) would make an individual rebel and quit on the spot. The analogy holds true for your dog. While pain avoidance works for some dogs, for others it creates a level of anxiety so high that learning cannot take place. The dog may even become hysterical. Pain avoidance training causes other dogs to put on the brakes and resist; training becomes a contest of wills between the dog and trainer.

Standard pain avoidance techniques are easy for the trainer to learn and can be applied more or less mechanically to the dog. Unfortunately, this mechanical application interferes with some people's ability to notice the effect the training is having on the dog. The technique is generally applied by rote, and the reaction of the dog is ignored. The owner continues to jerk on the dog's collar, never noticing that the dog is slinking and cringing around, and that the dog is becoming more and more anxious as training continues. Or, the owner fails to notice the dog becoming more sullen and resistant with every yank of the choke chain.

Inducive training tends to build confidence in the dog. The dog is prevented from making mistakes rather than punished. The dog is not afraid of the training or the trainer. As we will see, dogs are sometimes corrected in inducive training, but only when they have clearly demonstrated that they have made the association between the cue word and the desired behavior and have chosen not to perform. The type of correction administered varies with the nature of each dog. If the dog has been trained with the inducive method, when corrections are needed, they can be escalated in intensity until the dog accepts the fact that you *can* force him to respond. That is, you can start with verbal discipline, then move to a buckle collar correction, then to the pinch collar, and finally to the choke chain (see p. 33). Conversely, when a dog that has been trained only with pain

Fig. 3-1. Teaching the sit
with pain avoidance:
choke chain pulls on
dog's neck and handler
smacks dog's rear.

avoidance using a choke chain refuses to do something you know he is capable of doing, the only way to get tougher is to become violent. It may become necessary at some point in any training program to cause a dog pain in order to get the message across that you are in control, and the dog must do (or not do) certain things to coexist with you. However, starting a learning experience by deliberately causing a dog pain is unacceptable to me.

A dog who makes a mistake is not committing a crime. When a dog fails to do what you have trained him to do, he is not *bad*. He is merely *wrong*. I want to shape my dog's behavior in the most positive way I can, so that my dog will be a happy, confident, and secure companion, knowing what is expected of him and not constantly testing to see how much he can get away with.

There are a few drawbacks to the inducive method. It is slower than pain avoidance and requires more thought and more observation on the part of the trainer. Some dogs simply do not respond to food, play, or toys. Such dogs generally have been raised without a great deal of human contact, and don't know how to play, or they have temperament flaws which prevent them from responding. Sometimes a great deal of patience and affection can reverse the response of such a dog, and he can be taught to play and work for positive reward. If not, standard pain avoidance techniques can be used to bring the dog under control.

Most training uses a combination of pain avoidance and reward. With pain avoidance training, after the choke collar is snapped or pulled, the dog is usually praised. With inducive training, once the dog clearly understands what is expected of him and chooses not to do it, he is verbally and/or physically corrected. The difference between the two methods lies in when and how much each is used.

4

Who's in Charge Here, Anyway?

Dominance and *alpha behavior* are terms you will become familiar with as you continue to read this book. They are important concepts which every pet owner should comprehend. The dog is an animal, not a human being. By nature, he is a pack animal. Every pack has a leader, known as the *alpha* animal, that dominates and leads the others. The alpha is the boss who runs the show and makes decisions about what the pack will or won't do. The other members of the pack form a hierarchy of dominance and submission, meaning that someone is on top, and the rest of the group follows. Each animal knows his or her place in this hierarchy. The alpha dog may be either male or female. In your home, you and your family become your dog's pack. Any additional dogs you have are also part of the pack. It is *your* responsibility to establish *yourself* in the alpha position in your pack. If you do not do this, the dog will, *as a natural behavior*, attempt to fill the leadership void. If this happens, you are asking for trouble. Some examples: At one time, in the course of my work, I would regularly visit disabled people in their homes. In one home, three adults lived with a ten-pound Poodle. As I was visiting with my client, the Poodle came up and nudged my hand to be petted. As I stroked him, I happened to touch his collar. He bit me on the hand. My client apologized, saying, "Oh, he doesn't let us touch his collar because he thinks we might be planning to give him a bath." Three adults were ruled by a ten-pound dog who disliked baths.

A trainer of Basset Hounds received a telephone call from the owner of a young male Basset. The man indicated that in the evenings, if the dog was not ready to go to sleep, he would stand at the top of the stairs when the family tried to go up to bed and growl and show his teeth. The family would have to wait until the dog was ready before they could retire.

A young couple called me about their seven-year-old Alaskan Malamute (a large breed originally bred to pull sleds). They had a two-year-old child, and the dog had begun to growl at the baby when she came anywhere near him. This one hundred-pound dog had finally snapped at the two-year-old several times, prompting the phone call. I asked if the parents had ever disciplined the dog, especially when he was a youngster. "No," they replied, "we believed in letting him grow up naturally."

All of these dogs had moved into the alpha position in their packs, because the humans had failed to do so. All of these dogs were endangering the people they lived with, but *not one of* these was a vicious dog! Obviously, the risk was greatest in the case of the baby and the Malamute because of the size and power of the dog.

How can you tell if your dog is exhibiting dominant behavior and challenging you for the leadership of the pack? A normal dog that is trying to take over alpha position is not going to attack you savagely or try to rip your throat out. What he will do is test you, starting with fairly subtle behavior. For example:

> You call the dog to come to you. He looks you squarely in the eye, turns his back and saunters off in the other direction.

> The dog is chewing on something that is not his. You say, "No", wanting him to stop. He stares at you with a hard look until you look away. If you reach for the object, he raises his hackles (the hair on the back of his neck) and growls.

> You take the dog out for a walk on leash. If you attempt to restrain him, he takes the leash in his mouth, or hooks a foot over it.

> The dog is sitting in your favorite chair. You tell him to get out and he growls at you or lifts a lip to show his teeth.

> You tell the dog to do something and he snaps at you, deliberately missing by only inches.

Some other signs to look for: your dog growls or snaps if you try to take food or a toy away from him (sometimes if you just come near his dish while he is eating); the dog has chosen a particular spot in the house that is his, and threatens anyone who tries to move him; the dog growls or snaps when a certain part of his body is touched. Any of these behaviors indicate that the dog believes *he* is the pack leader, not you.

A good pack leader does not tolerate fights in his pack. If you own more than one dog and there are dog fights while you are present, you have a dominance problem. Frequently, dogs who urinate in the house, especially adolescent males, are establishing their own territory and declaring themselves alpha.

Most dogs will test their owners once or twice—usually in adolescence (between six and eighteen months, as the dog approaches sexual maturity). If the issue is settled when it first occurs, that is usually the end of the matter. It will probably reoccur if another dog is introduced into the family.

There is a difference between a lack of obedience training and a dominance problem, although the two are frequently related. A dog that does not mind because he has not been trained is different from a dog that does not mind because he

Fig. 4-1. *Don't overlook any challenge to your authority. Your dog should permit you to remove his food dish, even while he is eating. This does not mean you should tease the dog however.*

does not feel you have the authority to tell him what to do. Some obedience-trained dogs will continue to challenge their owners for alpha position on a regular basis. Some dogs are simply born to be alpha dogs, and have trouble accepting a lesser ranking no matter what kind of training they have. This can be found in any breed or mix of breeds, but is most common in the large breeds, such as the Doberman Pinscher, the Alaskan Malamute, the Rottweiler, the German Shepherd Dog, the Great Dane, and also in the Pembroke Welsh Corgi, a little dog who thinks big. Let me share an example with you. Tora is a male Akita. The Akita was bred in Japan for guard work, among other purposes. Pat, Tora's owner, has been training Tora for three years for obedience competition, and has done quite well with him as Tora is the only living male Akita to hold the advanced AKC obedience title of Utility Dog. About once a month, Pat will tell Tora to do something, and Tora will growl at her. Pat calmly proceeds to discipline him, and the issue is settled—for another month. In the hands of a less determined owner, Tora could be a real problem. Although he is one of the sweetest, most affectionate dogs I know, Tora is a strong alpha personality and the ongoing challenges are *normal* behavior for him. He is never allowed to win, however.

BECOMING THE ALPHA FIGURE

What should you do if you are challenged for dominance by your own dog? First of all, do not overlook, excuse, or dismiss any challenge. Remember, your dog is not being bad or vicious. This is *normal* behavior, especially if your dog is an adolescent. The more challenges you ignore because you are unwilling or afraid to make an issue of the behavior, the worse it will get. You must use judgment when you confront your dog. If the behavior has just started, or if the dog is fairly small relative to your size and strength, I recommend the "scruff-shake." The "scruff-shake" and the "takedown" correction I am about to describe are wonderfully effective in conveying the message, "I set the limits around here, buster," to your errant canine. They are natural corrections, similar to those the mother dog gives a pup that has stepped over the line or the discipline the alpha wolf gives to a pushy subordinate. They are not cruel.

The Scruff-Shake

Face the dog and grab him by the loose skin on either side of the neck. You can grab a small dog or puppy by the skin at the back of the neck, just behind the ears. Try to maintain eye contact. Lift his front feet off the floor and shake him—hard— from side to side, repeating the word "No!" in a firm low-pitched voice. If ten seconds of this appears sufficient, drop him unceremoniously and ignore him for at least ten minutes. DO NOT APOLOGIZE in any way. Do not pet him or speak to him or in any way try to make up with him. *The dog was wrong and deserved the correction.* It was given in physical language he can understand. If the dog has already had training, a fifteen to thirty minute down-stay (see p. 98) will reinforce your message of, "I am the alpha figure in this pack."

Fig. 4-2. *The scruff-shake. Glare at the dog and shake him from side to side.*

Fig. 4-3. *The scruff-shake at your eye level. Drop the dog unceremoniously when you are done.*

Now, if it is possible, try to set up the situation which provoked the dominance challenge in the first place (i.e., take the food away briefly, or haul the dog off the sofa or whatever). Do this without anger or malice, in a matter-of-fact way: "I am the head honcho, dog, and you might as well accept that." If the dog previously snapped at you, or if you are afraid he might, put on a heavy coat and gloves before trying this. When you repeat the behavior, if the dog accepts your discipline, fine. You may have resolved the issue permanently or it may crop up again. If the second go-round produces the same aggressive behavior, repeat the scruff-shake and follow it with the takedown.

The Takedown

This starts the same as the scruff-shake. After eight or ten good shakes, continue to hold the dog's neck, and pin him to the floor and hold him there, maintaining eye contact until the dog submits (see below). I have known dogs that had to be held in the takedown position as long as five minutes (although it will feel more like five hours) until the growling stopped. Some trainers, depending upon their weight, actually straddle the dog as they pin it to the ground. This enhances your message of physically dominating the animal. If at any time you become afraid, or if this seems overwhelming, seek professional help.

If you have repeatedly tried the scruff-shake and takedown without success, a harsher correction is in order. (Again, if you cannot physically do what I am about to describe, and your dog has not responded to the other dominance corrections, you need professional help.) Continue to hold the dog by the scruff of his neck and lift him to your eye level. If all four of his feet are off the ground, so much the better. Maintain eye contact, repeat the word "No!" in a low, gruff voice, and shake the dog hard from side to side. When the growling or snapping subsides, drop the dog abruptly and ignore him or put him on a long down as described above. Obviously, you will not drop a small dog from your eye level to the ground. Drop him about six inches from the ground, so the message, "I am the boss," comes across, but he is not injured by the fall. He should land hard enough to impress on him that you have won this round.

Fig. 4-4. The Take-Down.

You can unwittingly reward a dog's dominant behavior, thus making it more likely to be repeated. For example, when the dog growls inappropriately (either at you or at another person who is clearly not a threat), you pet the dog and reassure it, rather than disciplining it. This is often the start of a dominance problem. The owner becomes more and more afraid of the dog and either ends up allowing the dog to rule or gets rid of the dog.

SUBMISSION—WINNING THE BATTLE

A dog disciplined with a scruff-shake and/or takedown should show some physical signs of submission. He will avoid eye contact, fold his ears back, lick the air, and appear to grin or smile. His physical posture will be close to the ground with his tail tucked between his legs. He may even slink on his belly. As a still more submissive sign, the dog will lie on his back, tuck his tail and roll over to expose his groin. He may urinate. In wolves and wild dogs, this submissive behavior will automatically stop the aggression from the dominant animal. You should therefore take your cue from your dog, and back off as soon as he submits. Do not punish him if he urinated; he did

Fig. 4-5. Look for signs of submission: dog avoids eye contact, pins his ears back and tucks his tail.

not forget his housebreaking, he was saying "I give up, you win." Do ignore him for a while after he submits, or use the down-stay described in the training section.

WARNING: There is a big difference between establishing alpha position with a young dog, a small dog, or a trained dog, and trying to take the alpha position away from a large dog that has firmly established his or her leadership in your pack. If you are now aware that you have such a problem, seek professional help from an experienced trainer or behaviorist immediately. Do not take on such a dog alone. Even if you have a smaller dog and you are afraid of the dog, seek professional help. Don't be embarrassed to admit you cannot physically control your dog, but *do* get some help. Several years ago, the largest dog I have ever seen dragged his ninety pound owner into my beginner's class. Charlie was a sweet dog, but he was just over a year old and I could see the signs that he was ready to assert his challenge for leadership. I put a training collar on Charlie and tried to get him to perform a few simple exercises. Charlie did not care to move, and I could not budge him. I spoke to his owner about having her husband, who was much stronger physically, handle the dog. She asked him, but he was too busy, and besides, he could control Charlie without much trouble. Reluctantly, I insisted Charlie leave the class, as I knew if there were a showdown, Charlie would win and someone might get hurt. I recommended another physically stronger trainer, but the woman was not interested. As far as I know, she took the dog home, where the pecking order is still: Husband, Charlie, Wife. You must know your own limits.

There is one recommendation I make to the owner of every dog who has an ongoing dominance problem when one or two confrontations do not put an end to the struggle—neutering. Spay the female, castrate the male. Frequently, within a few months the problem simply disappears. It would seem that as the sex related hormones leave the bloodstream, the alpha issues lose their importance to the dog. This does not mean the dog becomes a snivelling wimp. The dog maintains his or her own personality, but merely ceases to vie for leadership. In some cases, the "cure" is fast and complete; in others, the behavior diminishes but does not disappear completely. I have rarely seen neutering fail to have a positive effect on a dominance problem, even on a dog as old as seven years.

WHY NOT PAIN AVOIDANCE?

If training with food and play is so wonderful, why doesn't everyone do it? Why do three-quarters of the obedience books on the book store or library shelf insist that food training is bad and that the dog who is trained with food will be unreliable and will not respect its owner?

The standard pain avoidance techniques used by many trainers today were originally designed for training dogs for the military. The dogs chosen for this purpose were big, tough and aggressive and tolerated a great deal of rough physical discipline. Those who could not tolerate the discipline were washed out of the program and replaced by other big, tough,

aggressive dogs. The training methods were designed to produce results as fast as possible, and no one cared very much
about the dogs' response, as long as they did what they were
told. These were not housepets.

Pain avoidance training was eventually popularized for pet
dogs all over the country. The method was fast and effective
and easy for people to learn (when in doubt, jerk on the choke
collar). People saw their unruly animals learn to obey, and they
believed the trainers who told them that food rewards would
make the dogs unreliable. If some dogs also learned to cringe
and slink whenever they saw their owners pick up the collar
and leash, the owners were told that there was something wrong
with the dogs, never that the training method might be inappropriate. Over the years, the myths about positive reward training perpetuated themselves and the few people who dared to
question the negative results of pain avoidance training were
dismissed as "bleeding hearts." Those people who did choose
to use positive reward methods were dismissed as not being
serious about training and were actually called names in print
("cookie-pusher" and "sissy" being the milder names). The
problem has been that pain avoidance trainers, because the
method is so mechanical, have rarely bothered to learn much
about dog psychology. They frequently do not understand
dominance and the pack leader concept. They confuse respect
for the owner with fear of the owner. They refuse to believe that
a dog can really enjoy training and still respect its owner; dogs
work only because the owner gives them no choice. One pain
avoidance trainer told me that no dog could work with both
joy and precision, and he preferred to sacrifice the joy.

We have seen that this is not true. Your dog will respect
you if you have established yourself as the pack leader; the
alpha. Once that relationship is in place, the method used to
train the various obedience exercises is immaterial.

As far as reliability is concerned, many dogs trained with
positive reward methods are regular winners in obedience trials,
and make delightful house pets as well. Furthermore, wild
animals trained for circuses and theme park attractions are
almost always trained with the use of food rewards. Would you
care to try to put a choke collar on Shamu, the killer whale?

These animals must perform reliably, as their trainers' incomes—and sometimes their personal safety—depend on it.

Pain avoidance training is neither bad nor wrong. It is effective with some dogs and is a fast, mechanical method for teaching a dog to obey. It is not a way I choose to relate to my dogs. Positive reward training builds confidence in the dog, minimizes the dog's anxiety, fear and resentment and teaches the dog to obey. It makes the *process* of training as important as the result—a learning experience for both dog and owner. Positive reward training is a vehicle for establishing two-way communication. And it's fun! Who said dog training had to be a grim contest of wills?

5

Before
You Begin
Training

Now that you understand the basic canine learning process, and the difference between pain avoidance and positive reward training, let us examine how to reward desirable behavior (thereby encouraging the dog to do it again) and how to stop or correct behavior you wish to eliminate.

Rewards

How do you reward a dog? Always use verbal praise and petting as your principal form of reward, along with food, toys, or play. Verbal praise as a training tool is discussed on page 56. More information on how to use praise as you teach each behavior appears in the next chapter.

Food is another good reward. Generally, food used in training should be something other than the dog's regular food. I have trained dogs using everything from cheese to Cheerios. Whatever you use, it should be cut or broken into small pieces (no bigger than a dime) before your training session. I prefer something soft like cheese or generic hot dogs which the dog can swallow quickly, rather than something crunchy like dog biscuits that the dog has to stop and chew, thereby distracting him from the lesson at hand. If the dog becomes overly excited about the food, do not panic. Keep trying to work with whatever type of food you originally chose for a few days. If the dog figures out that the food will continue to appear his excitement may lessen and he will begin to concentrate. If not, try something less tasty—go from cheese to his regular dry food. Given some time, most dogs calm down and accept food rewards matter-of-factly. What about the opposite problem, the dog that is not interested in the treat? Try a variety of treats, including some of the commercially prepared treats available at the grocery store. If nothing seems to interest your dog, try withholding his food for twenty-four hours. He will not starve in that time period, I promise you. If none of these things work, you will have to substitute play, or toys, or use praise alone to reward your dog.

Food rewards always come from the trainer's hand. The dog is never allowed to get food from the ground. If you drop a treat and the dog lunges for it, restrain him with the collar and leash and a firm "No!" Then pick up the treat and hand it to him. This keeps the dog's attention on you and prevents him from spending part of each training session playing vacuum cleaner, searching for any dropped goodies.

Some dogs will perk up for particular toys, especially those that squeak. If you use squeaky toys in your training, do not give them to the dog as everyday playthings. Be careful when giving the dog a squeaky toy that he does not chew the squeaker out and swallow it. Soft vinyl toys, available at better pet shops, are preferable to hard vinyl toys as they stretch more and are harder to destroy. When the dog has chewed a hole in the toy,

Fig. 5-1. *An assortment of my dog's favorite squeaky toys.*

dispose of it and buy a new one to prevent him from swallowing all the pieces. Use the toy to get the dog's attention and let him have it to chew on and play with for a few seconds as a reward.

For dogs that like to retrieve, a Frisbee, a ball, or a boat bumper (canvas covered cork float) can be used. Start the session by having the dog retrieve a few times, then use the retrieving object as the food and the squeaky toy are used. The dog's reward will be the opportunity to retrieve.

As you proceed with training, you will gradually withdraw the additional reward (other than praise) and offer it only on an occasional basis. Begin withdrawing the reward when the dog has clearly made the association between the cue word and the desired behavior. The reward should never disappear completely, however, as the dog will always benefit from occasional extra positive reinforcement for doing what he is told. Praise will *always* be given.

CORRECTIONS

In many cases, a correction can simply be a verbal reminder, possibly spoken in a firmer voice. "**Sit!**," not merely "Sit." When you administer a physical correction to your dog (other than a dominance correction) you will do so by putting quick pressure on his collar and then releasing that pressure.

For most training purposes I recommend the plain buckle collar. As we will discover in the section on training procedures, however, some dogs do require more physical firmness. For those dogs who cannot be controlled with a buckle collar, I recommend the collar shown in Figure 53. This is variously known as a pinch collar, a German training collar or a pronged collar. It looks like a medieval torture instrument, but is in fact more humane than the traditional choke chain. *Fitted properly,* this collar delivers *a mild pinch* to the dog's neck which communicates your control effectively to even the toughest dogs and cannot physically damage the dog. It is especially useful for very heavily coated dogs and for dogs with heavily muscled necks, such as Rottweilers and Boxers, who simply do not feel the directions given with a buckle collar. Pinch collars come

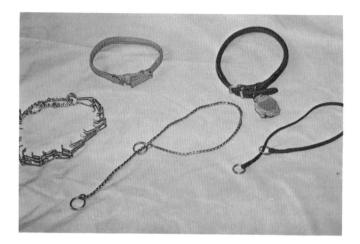

Fig. 5-2. Collars. Clockwise from lower left: A pinch collar for smaller dogs, a nylon buckle collar, a rolled leather collar with tags taped together, a nylon choke collar, a chain choke collar.

Fig. 5-3. A correctly fitted pinch collar. Remember, when the training session is over, remove the collar.

in different weights and can also be used on small dogs that do not respond to the buckle collar. The collar is worn high on the neck and is fitted by adding or removing links. Notice that the collar is constructed so that the pinching effect is limited. If you find you need such a collar and are disturbed by its looks, try one on your own arm before putting it on the dog. Again, it is essential that it fit snugly just under the ears.

The choke collar or slip collar has long been the traditional obedience collar. I believe it is the cruelest collar you can use because it works to whip across the dog's trachea, actually cutting off his air quite painfully (hence the name "choke" collar). If it is not put on the dog correctly or if it is kept tight by pressure on the leash it will cause constant choking. If used improperly on a small or young dog, I believe it can cause permanent physical damage to the vertebrae in the neck. Some dogs have pulled against a choke collar for so long that they have learned to ignore the pain and it has no effect on them. If you must use a choke chain to control your dog, be aware you will be causing him pain. As we have seen, pain avoidance is one way to force a dog to obey. Therefore, if you are going to apply pain avoidance with the choke collar, you should do it as efficiently and as effectively as possible. The thinner the choke chain, the more pain I believe it causes so use the thinnest choke chain which will hold the dog so you can quickly get the message across: "If you do not do as I want, dog, I will cause you pain."

Fig. 5-4. A correctly fitted choke collar.

The choke chain should just go over the dog's head, and should ride as high as possible on his neck. (See the section on pain avoidance training for more information.) There are very few dogs which cannot be trained on the buckle collar, and fewer still that need the choke chain.

WARNING: Never leave a pinch or a choke collar on an unattended dog. The dog can get the ring of the collar caught on something and strangle. Neither collar is safe nor appropriate for an everyday dog collar.

Fig. 5-5. *The correct way to put on a chain collar for pain avoidance corrections. Be sure the choking or live ring comes across the top of the dog's neck or the collar will not release after you pull on it.*

There is a new device based on the design of a horse's bridle which is being used in some areas of the country. It is known as the "K-9 Kumalong" and is a mild pain avoidance device. Some trainers have had marked success controlling very large dogs with the Kumalong. I have not had any personal experience with this device, but if you have a very large dog or a dog that has had a neck or back injury, it might be worth looking into. You can obtain more information about the Kumalong by writing to Altru, Inc., P.O. Box 340, Sandia Park, New Mexico, 87047.

Administering A Correction

As previously stated, the simplest correction is verbal. Repeat the cue word in a firmer voice. You may need to accompany the repeated cue word with physical manipulation of the dog. Instead of gently positioning a dog that you are sure understands the word "Sit," position the dog abruptly. I do *not* mean you should hit or strike the dog. Just be a bit quicker

Fig. 5-6. The Kumalong.

with your actions, the message to the dog being "Hurry up! Do it now!" The next step up in this escalating scale of correction is the collar correction. A collar correction can be given with any of the three collars: buckle, pinch, or choke chain. *The correction consists of a quick pull or snap of the collar on the dog's neck, and then the pressure is immediately released.* The pressure on the dog's neck should last no longer than one tick of a clock. When done with the buckle collar it is more of a physical directing of the dog than an incident of pain avoidance. This is sufficient for most dogs. If you need to make more of a physical impression on the dog, first try the pinch collar and then the choke chain. Remember that any correction done with these collars is pain avoidance training. Be certain that any snap of the collar is followed by an *immediate* release of pressure on the dog's neck. With most dogs, the snap of the collar is done with a motion of the trainer's wrist. (See illustration.) Try this on yourself by slipping the dog's collar over your arm. Notice that a quick snap moves your arm more effectively than a long pull. A long pull tends to cause resistance on the part of the pullee (your arm or your dog). Your message to the dog should be that the pain stops when the behavior is done to your satisfaction.

Fig. 5-7. A traditional pain avoidance correction given by tightening the choke chain and then immediately releasing the pressure so the collar is slack on the dog's neck.

When Should You Correct Your Dog?

Before you administer a correction you must be sure your dog understands what is expected of him. How do you know that the dog is choosing not to do what he had been told, rather than failing to understand? Watch for behavioral signs that tell you the dog is catching on. In teaching the sit or the down, for example, if the dog hears the cue word and begins to assume the position before you can guide him, he is making the association between the cue word and the desired behavior. He is not yet secure in his understanding at this point. When the dog is responding reliably to the cue word alone (followed by reward), you can assume he understands.

For many dogs, the best correction is no correction. When the dog makes a mistake, simply withhold praise and reward, and help the dog to repeat the behavior correctly. For example, if you say, "Rover, sit," and the dog lies down, do not jerk him roughly into a sitting position. Rather, take a few steps forward to get him on his feet, repeat "Rover, sit," and physically manipulate him into a sit, then praise, reward, and repeat. If this is a new exercise, the dog may not have formed a firm association between the cue word and the behavior. If you are reasonably certain—through your observation — that the dog has made the association, try withholding praise and reward a few times before administering a correction. A dog that has been trained with positive reward methods will figure out fairly quickly that he has done something wrong when he is not rewarded.

However, there are times when the dog clearly does not care if you reward him or not. He simply chooses to do something other than what he was told. When this dog fails to respond to the cue word, that is the time to administer a mild correction. When you do administer a correction, you will know whether or not it was effective by observing the dog's response.

Effective Correction—If you say "Sit" to a dog that has previously demonstrated an understanding of the cue word, and the dog does not sit, administer a correction, starting with the least physical force, that will make him sit. Release the dog from the sit and repeat the cue word. If the dog responds correctly, reward him. The correction was well-timed and had the desired effect: "Yes dog, you *must* do this."

Corrected Too Soon—If the dog shows submissive behavior (see page 26) and appears anxious, the correction was badly timed and he needs to be gently shown again what is expected. Remember that a dog's learning pattern generally includes a number of retrogressions or backsliding incidents, in which he simply blanks out a behavior he knew perfectly two days before. Correction at this time will only confuse him, not improve his performance.

Ineffective Correction—If you correct the dog, and he shows no signs of anxiety of submission, but does not do the behavior correctly the second time, your correction was well-timed but not effective. Next time get physically tougher with the dog. The particulars will be discussed for each exercise in the following chapter.

Aggressive Reaction—If you administer a correction and the dog reacts by growling or snapping at you, you do not have an obedience problem, you have a dominance problem. Administer a scruff-shake and/or takedown as explained in Chapter 4. When the dominance issue has been settled — even if only temporarily — return to your training session and proceed from the point at which you had the set-to.

An aggressive reaction can be provoked by an overly harsh correction. Therefore, it is important that you start with the least physically violent correction and only progress to tougher corrections when you are sure a) the dog understands what is expected and b) the gentler correction is not sufficient. If you are not sure, err in the dog's favor. That is, gently show the dog what you want again and prevent him from making a mistake. Repeat the gentler correction several times if necessary before using a harsher method.

Obviously the timing of a correction requires judgment, patience and observation of the dog. Some dogs need a firm hand until they accept the fact that the training is going to happen and they'd best learn to live with it. This is clearly an issue linked to dominance. Remember that like Tora the Akita, some dogs keep testing their owners. Once the dog has accepted the idea that he must obey, training with the positive reward method usually can be accomplished with only an occasional need for physical correction. On the other hand, some dogs can barely tolerate any correction at all. One dog was so sensitive that if I even raised my voice to him, he would fall on the ground in a "don't beat me" attitude and scream. Dogs who react this way have faulty temperaments (this dog did). Most dogs fall somewhere in the middle of this continuum and will benefit from an appropriate, well-timed correction. Again, a dog that refuses to obey, either because he does not want to or because there is something else he would rather do, is not being bad. He is merely making a wrong choice *from your point of view.* Corrections should be administered without anger. Correction is not punishment because the dog was bad; it is simply a more physically forceful way to strengthen the association between a cue word and the desired behavior.

Proof-Training

A dog who is proof-trained on a particular behavior will perform that behavior under any and all circumstances. In our training program, we will use proof-training after we are certain the dog has mastered an obedience exercise, so that he will behave reliably, no matter what is going on.

When teaching your dog something new, eliminate as many distractions as possible. Take the dog to a quiet place, either in your home or in your fenced yard. Ideally, there should be no other people or animals around. After the dog has learned the behavior to your satisfaction in a quiet area, you will begin proof-training. This means you will ask the dog to perform the behavior under increasingly more distracting circumstances. After the initial training with minimal distractions your next step will be to provide a few temptations to make the work a little more difficult for the dog. You might work in a park, but at some distance from other people. Be prepared to back up to the previous training level each time you introduce new distractions, so that the dog will have every opportunity to do the exercise correctly. For example, even though your dog will lie down and stay successfully for five minutes with you all the way across your family room, when you take him to an isolated area in the park, begin by standing next to him and reduce the length of the stay period. Gradually work up to the level you had reached in the initial quiet area. Then increase the level of distraction again. This time, you may want to work right next to a softball game or playground. Always back up to the point in training where you are pretty sure the dog understands and is able to do what is expected without making a mistake. Next, you might work on a busy sidewalk or in front of a grocery store.

A word of caution about working in public. While the dog needs discipline when and where it misbehaves, a tough physical correction and certainly a dominance correction given in front of a number of people is likely to draw some negative comments, or at least some dirty looks. I once got into a dominance struggle with a cute little Shetland Sheepdog while training in the park. He bit me twice, and as I had him in the takedown position, I looked up and noticed some older ladies who had been watching. Their former sweet smiles at the cute little dog quickly turned to black looks at the nasty trainer who was "abusing" the poor creature. I heard muttered comments of "Humane Society" and "Call the Police." We left the park in a hurry and settled the dominance issue at home before venturing out to train again. But, when the dog is deliberately disobedient you must reinforce the point that he must perform as directed under any and all circumstances. Proof-training should continue to be as positive as possible, with minimal correction.

Fig. 5-8. Physical corrections administered in public can cause negative responses from other people.

6

Training Aids and Tips

Numerous factors affect your success as a trainer and your dog's ability to learn. Your expectations, attitudes, techniques, and skill in using various training equipment are some of the factors involved.

THE TRAINER

Your voice is one of your most important training tools. It can encourage the dog, excite him, reinforce him, or stop him. As you work with your dog you will speak to him in a pleasant conversational tone. Verbal correction should be given in a low-pitched firm voice. There is never a need to shout at your dog although there may be great temptation. Commands should be given quietly and should be statements, not questions. "Sit." not "Sit?" (As in, "Gee, I wish you'd sit. Please sit. Won't you sit?"). You are *telling* the dog to do something, not asking if he'd care to do it at his leisure. When you really want to let the dog know he has done well, use a high-pitched, excited tone and tell the dog how good he is. Don't be embarrassed about talking to your dog. Train in a secluded place until you feel comfortable using your voice to let the dog know just how he is doing. I have trained my dogs in parks, on the sidewalks, and in shopping malls, talking all the time, and so far no one has sent for the men in the white coats! I have only received a few indulgent smiles. Your body posture also conveys messages to your dog. When a dog is attempting to dominate another dog, he will stand high on his toes to look taller, and if the other dog is submitting he will drop his head and tail to look smaller. When you are teaching new behaviors to your dog, you can defuse his anxiety by presenting a lower profile. Do not loom or bend over your dog unless you are having a dispute about dominance. With a puppy or a timid dog, squat down or kneel frequently when teaching a new behavior.

Another important training "tool" is consistency. Once you have read this book, you are one step ahead of your dog. You know how the finished behavior will look. The dog is starting from ground zero, without this information. It is important to keep your commands consistent, especially during initial training. The dog does not speak English, so "down" and "lie down" are two completely unrelated terms to him. Choose a word and stick to it or your dog will be unnecessarily confused. Similarly, it is best that only one person do the initial training. "Come" from you sounds different to the dog than "Come" from your spouse or child. Eventually the dog should learn to accept commands from all members of the family, but first give him a chance to make a solid connection between the desired behavior and the command as spoken by only one person.

Patience is another vital training "tool." Unless you are a candidate for sainthood, your level of patience will vary from day to day. If you have had a stressful day and are feeling angry with the world, you probably had better skip the dog training. Take the dog out and play a game or just take a walk instead. If you do find yourself losing patience with the dog, don't continue the session, grimly determined that he must do a particular behavior correctly before you can quit. Stop as soon as you feel your temper rising and put the dog away. There is always another day to accomplish your training goals.

What if you do lose your temper with the dog? Try to stop as soon as possible and separate yourself from the dog. You may shake his confidence for a while, but if it is not a regular occurrence the dog will recover. At the next session, back up a few steps in your training to something you know he can do and avoid any correction until he is working happily again. Dogs have their off days too, so either or both of you may have a low frustration tolerance on any given day. Give the dog the benefit of the doubt and back off for a day if he appears unusually uncooperative.

Here is a suggestion to help prevent your becoming impatient. When you have had a frustrating session with your dog and have finally gotten him to perform after some struggle, it is tempting to repeat the problem exercise one last time to be sure the lesson has been driven home. *Don't do it.* Stop with even partial success while you still have control of your temper, praise the dog and quit. If it was a particularly trying session, separate yourself from the dog, but if you still have a sense of humor left, play with the dog to relieve the tension you both feel.

THE EQUIPMENT

Collars

My own dogs, and all dogs in my beginning classes, receive their initial training on plain, buckle collars of leather or nylon. If the dog wears the collar all the time and there are identification tags attached, the tags should be taped together so they do not rattle in the dog's ear constantly. The collar should fit comfortably; just tight enough so that you can easily run a finger between the collar and the dog's neck.

Leashes

The type of leash you should buy depends on the amount of use it will get. If you walk your dog on a leash several times a day, the quality is important. If you only use a leash to take the dog to the vet a few times a year, anything that will keep the dog attached to you will do. You will need a leash for teaching the obedience exercises in this book. I recommend either a four-foot or a six-foot leash of leather or soft nylon or cotton webbing. Plastic leashes, nylon webbed leashes and chain leashes can hurt your hands if the dog pulls suddenly. Also, the chain leash can catch in the dog's ear or coat and pull painfully. Use the lightest weight leash that will hold your dog securely. If you have a small dog, be especially careful that the snap of the leash is as small as possible so the dog will not be smacked in the face when the leash is attached to his collar. You will need a long, light line to teach some of the exercises in this book. A long line is simply a piece of cord about thirty feet in length. If you have a small dog, use very light nylon cord or string or even twine. Use a heavier cord for a larger dog. If

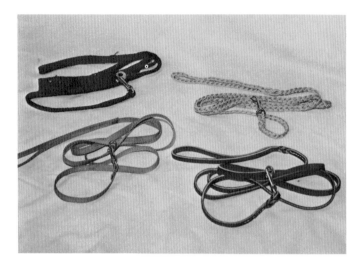

Fig. 6-1. Leashes. Clockwise from lower left. Flat nylon
(hard on the hands if you have a big dog who is pulling);
rolled nylon; braided nylon; leather.

you wish, you may buy a bolt snap of appropriate size and tie
it to one end of the line. If this is too elaborate for your tastes,
simply tie the line to the dog's collar.

SPECIAL TRAINING CIRCUMSTANCES

Appearances to the contrary, not all little dogs are sweet
and not all big dogs are potential killers. Training a very small
or a very large dog presents some unique problems.

Training Toy Dogs

Dogs classified as toy breeds weigh less than fifteen pounds
(when the dog is at its proper weight) and stand less than ten
inches tall at the shoulder. People who own toy dogs sometimes
forget that they are really dogs and allow them to be tiny tyrants,
growling and snapping at people and generally ruling the house.
There is a fine line between cute and obnoxious. Many spoiled
little dogs cross that line and become real nuisances, if not to
their indulgent owners, then to everyone else who comes in
contact with them. Toy dogs need obedience training. They

Fig. 6-2. Little dogs can be as
badly behaved as large dogs.

deserve to have consistent limits set for their behavior so that
they do not become midget monsters. Don't believe for a minute
that you cannot have a dominance problem with that cute little
half-pint canine. The difference in having a dominance problem
with a Chihuahua and a Doberman is merely in the extent of
damage each can cause. A snappy toy dog can be dangerous
to children. The worst bite I ever received in training class came
from a precious little ten-pound dog who really wanted to kill
me. Had a larger dog displayed that degree of viciousness, I
might have had permanent, serious injury.

Training toy dogs can be physically harder on the trainer
than on the dog because it is difficult to reach the little ones.
Therefore, the initial training of a toy, especially the sit, down,
and stand, should be done with the dog on a table. This enables
the trainer to position the dog for best eye contact, which is
the starting point for all training. Putting the toy on the table
also prevents the natural tendency to loom over a small dog,
and is much easier on the trainer's back and knees. Use the
kitchen table or a desk or counter top. Clear off all distracting
items and put a towel or, preferably, a rubber bathmat on the
table so the dog will have firm footing. Table training can be
used for any of the smaller breeds up to the size of a Cocker
Spaniel or Shetland Sheepdog. It is also useful in working with
low slung heavier dogs such as Corgis and Bassets, if you have
a steady table to put them on (and can lift them onto the table).
Once he makes the association between cue word and behavior,
put the little guy on the floor to work with him. Minimize

bending over the toy as this will not only cause anxious, submissive behavior, but can set up a pattern in which the dog tries to keep distance between you. If you must give a collar correction to a small dog, keep his size in mind and adjust the amount of force you use accordingly. In the first few sessions of an obedience class, you can frequently observe the "flying toy" syndrome, especially in classes which teach by pain avoidance.

Training Extremely Large Dogs

Working with a giant breed—one that stands twenty-eight inches or more at the shoulders and/or weighs more than one hundred pounds—is a whole different ball game. Even with the positive reward method, training one of these bruisers requires muscle and timing. The first giant breed I ever worked with was an Irish Wolfhound. This dog's shoulder came well above my waist and I am sure he weighed more than one hundred pounds. I was able to get his front end to do what I wanted, but the back end seemed to function independently. I gained instant respect for the woman who was training him.

The best advice I can give the owner of a giant breed is to start working with the dog as a young puppy. (See the section on puppy training for specifics.) These dogs get big so fast, it is often difficult to remember they are puppies with limited

Fig. 6-3. Training a full-grown giant breed requires timing, muscle and long arms!

attention spans. Remember to keep training sessions short and positive. If you begin working with the dog when it is a puppy you will be able to teach the exercises which require physical manipulation much more easily because you will be able to reach both ends of the dog simultaneously. If you are a small person or lack physical strength and have an adult giant breed, you may need some help to teach the initial behaviors. If necessary, two people can physically manipulate the dog. If you have a dominance problem with an adult giant breed dog, I strongly urge you to seek professional help. It can be extremely dangerous to struggle for alpha position with a dog who is much stronger than you are and that may outweigh you. Arrange for some private instruction from a competent, physically strong instructor and settle the issue before you attempt any training.

Children as Dog Trainers

Children tend to have lower levels of frustration tolerance than adults. The combination of child and puppy may make an appealing picture, but as a training setup it can spell poten-

Fig. 6-4. Children and dogs are appealing together, but are not an ideal training team.

tial disaster. Some children lack the innate authority to enforce discipline on a dog. That is, even a child who has the required patience may not be able to impose his or her will on a dog. The older the child, the more likely he or she will be to have success as a dog trainer. I have worked with a few children under the age of ten who were competent trainers, but they were in the minority. It would be best in most cases for an adult to do the initial training and then show the child how to give the dog commands. Children and dogs are ideal playmates as long as the child understands that the dog is a living, feeling creature and as long as the dog is not contending with the child for attention from the adults in the family.

The High or Low Energy Dog

If you have a high-energy dog or a young dog that is confined most of the day, he may need a run or a session of ball-chasing to work off some steam before training. On the other hand, if a dog is with you all day or is not particularly enthusiastic about training, you may need to confine him or isolate him for an hour or two before your training session so that he will be more eager to participate and enjoy your attention. This is also effective with a dog that continues to push you for alpha position.

Weather Considerations

Take the weather into consideration when you plan a training session. If your dog has very little coat and spends most of his time indoors, it would be better to avoid training outside when it is very cold. It is difficult for the dog to concentrate when he is shaking and shivering. Conversely, when the weather is very warm, a heavily-coated dog will be uncomfortable. Dogs can suffer from heatstroke or just be less willing to concentrate when the temperature goes up. Schedule your summer training sessions early in the morning or in the evening. Be especially careful in the heat if you have a dog with a short muzzle (what some people call the pushed-in face dogs). These include Pugs, Pekingese, Boxers, Bulldogs and mixes of these breeds. They can experience difficulty breathing if overheated.

Fig. 6-5. *Training is more fun when the dog is comfortable. Have your short-coated dog wear a sweater when it's cold out.*

Fig. 6-6. *Thickly coated dogs overheat quickly in warm weather. Train them very early while it is cool, or find an air conditioned place to work.*

The Shaggy-headed Dog

If you have a dog whose hair covers his eyes, either cut the hair over the eyes short or keep it tied back. It is not true that these breeds have more sensitive eyes than others. Your dog cannot see through a face full of hair any more than you can, and may become touchy and irritable because he frequently can't see what is coming at him. Seeing your dog's eyes is an important part of training, as you will learn.

TRAINING CLASSES

You may prefer to train your dog in a group situation. The benefits of attending a *good* beginning obedience class are that explanations and demonstrations can be given repeatedly until the handlers understand, and that the dog learns to obey even around other dogs and people and a degree of chaos. The key word here is "good." A class is only as good as the instructor who runs it. There are no licensing bodies or regulatory agencies controlling obedience trainers. Anyone who can persuade other people to pay him or her for lessons can become a dog trainer. How can you find a good training class? Call the instructor and ask if only one method is used for all dogs in the class or whether methods are suited to the individual dogs. There is no one method suitable for all dogs. Beware of the inflexible instructor who claims otherwise. If you have any thoughts of going on to more advanced training, ask the instructor about his or her experience in obedience competition. Ask how many different dogs and different breeds of dogs the instructor has personally trained. Listen for references to AKC obedience degrees: C.D. (Companion Dog), C.D.X. (Companion Dog Excellent), U.D. (Utility Dog), O.T.Ch. (Obedience Trial Champion). Not all competent instructors compete in obedience trials, but many do. If I wanted to train my dog beyond the most basic level, I would be very careful to choose an instructor who had personally taken a dog through the most advanced (U.D.) level. Unfortunately, training a dog—or even several dogs— to that level does not guarantee a high quality of instruction.

Go and observe the classes without your dog before you sign up. Any competent instructor will be willing to allow you to do this. Look for a reasonable student/instructor ratio. Is there at least one assistant available to work with a dog and handler who are having difficulty with the lesson? A few instructors are able to handle large classes alone, but they are rare. Ideally, a class of ten or more should have one principal instructor and at least one assistant. The more dogs, the more assistants. See if all of the dogs are being trained identically. Remember, a competent instructor modifies his or her methods to suit the dog. Most instructors have a standard method for teaching each behavior and then have several alternate methods for use if the standard method does not work with a particular dog. If you see an owner struggling with his or her dog, and the instructor continues to insist there is only one way to teach the exercise, look elsewhere for a training class. Do the people and dogs look like they are enjoying themselves? No one enjoys a class where the atmosphere is grim. Like the dogs, we thrive on praise and reward. Watch the instructor interact with the dogs. Is the treatment rough? (I am not referring to handling an aggressive dog.) Does the instructor or assistant work with the owner until he or she can get the dog to perform as desired? Don't be overly impressed that the *instructor* can get a student's dog to perform; that is to be expected. Can he or she teach the *owner* to control the dog—that is the mark of competence. Remember, the instructor isn't going to be around during practice sessions at home, so the owner must know what to do when he or she leaves the training area. Some instructors make claims that sound wonderful: they guarantee off-leash control in so many weeks. I judged a graduation from a beginner's class where this guarantee was made. Out of a class of fifteen, two dogs were under fairly good control off-leash. Half a dozen others bolted

Fig. 6-7. Nobody enjoys a training class where the atmosphere is punitive.

out the door as soon as the leash was removed, much to the embarrassment of their owners. The rest looked confused and anxious (and so did the owners). I asked the instructor about the guarantee and was told it meant they could repeat the class at a reduced fee. There is no way to predict with absolute certainty that a particular dog will learn a specific behavior or set of behaviors in a predetermined time. Dogs learn at different rates, so setting unrealistic expectations frustrates owners and ultimately can make obedience training a negative experience for the dog. Beware of guarantees and question them closely.

Sending the Dog Away for Training

Some people send their dogs to a kennel or to a professional trainer for training, rather than doing it themselves. Generally, this produces a dog that will obey the trainer at the trainer's kennel. Even if the owner spends one or two sessions with the trainer and dog, comprehension of the training process will be minimal and he will have limited success in transferring the training to the home front. The dog may well require periodic "tune-ups," which may or may not add to the cost of the training. Furthermore, the owner who sends his dog away for training really cannot be sure how the animal is being treated. Unlike the kids who can theoretically write home from camp or boarding school, your dog has no way to let you know if he is being subjected to abusive methods, in spite of what the trainer may have told you about the training methods used. The only situation in which I believe it makes sense to send a dog off for training is in the case of the firmly established alpha dog you are physically unable to dominate. Even then, I would recommend you go and observe the training sessions and insist on participating as soon as it is safe for you to do so.

7

Before You Pick up the Leash

As you and your dog learn each of the exercises in the next few chapters, you will accomplish more than changing the dog's behavior. You will also build a relationship with your dog based on mutual affection, respect, and trust. You will learn to read the body language of your dog. He already knows much of your body language as he has spent his whole life observing you. The dog will learn how to learn and will understand the limits you are now clearly giving him. He will learn to concentrate, building endurance like an athlete builds muscle.

When you start these training sessions, keep them short. Five to ten minutes twice a day should be sufficient for an adult dog. As the dog learns more behaviors, you may increase to one thirty-minute session per day. The dog will learn to concentrate for longer periods of time. Remember to intersperse treats and play with the work sessions. Try to work every day on a new behavior until the dog begins to show you that he understands what the cue word means. As you move on to proof training, continue to work at least four days per week. If you miss more than two consecutive days of training, be sure to back up one or two steps to something the dog knows well. Once the dog has been completely proof trained on an exercise and will perform to your satisfaction under any conditions you can contrive, work on that exercise no more than twice a week. Even after the dog has learned all of the exercises in these chapters you will have to work him once a week to keep him sharp. If you are applying the exercises to everyday situations, such as having the dog do a down-stay while you eat dinner, you should not need additional training sessions.

How long will it take for your dog to learn these exercises? That depends on your dog's age, willingness, and intelligence, and on your coordination, timing, and regularity of practice. All dogs learn at different rates. A dog may catch on quickly to some exercises but have difficulty with others. Do not set timetables for your dog. If you are working with him regularly, he will learn as fast as he can. Don't expect your dog to learn at the same rate as any other dog you have worked with. Relax and enjoy the training on a day-to-day basis. Remember that if you have a dominance issue to settle with your dog, that must be dealt with before you can make much progress in training.

As we look at each exercise, I will first explain how to teach the behavior to the dog using positive reward and preventing mistakes, then suggest ways to proof-train the exercise. Next, you will be shown how to correct the dog if necessary. And finally, ways to apply the training to your everyday life and interactions with the dog will be outlined. Please read the entire section on training before starting to work with your dog. By understanding all of the exercises you will have a better perspective on how to proceed with his training. Before you teach a particular exercise, reread the instructions to be sure you understand not only what you must do, but what to expect from your dog. To make explanations simpler, I have invented a medium-sized dog for you and named him Louis (or Louise, if you prefer). You and Louis will be taken through all of the steps for each exercise.

Put on Louis's well-fitted buckle collar and attach the leash. If Louis's collar has tags on it, tape them together so they don't rattle in his ear. The point where the collar and leash meet is called *the control point.* As you teach Louis new behaviors, you will hold the control point to give you the best possible leverage to position his body. Have your treats or toys ready and accessible. You may want to use a pouch attached to your belt or a plastic bag and a clothespin as in Figure 7.2. Praise and treats must be given *immediately* to be effective in rewarding the behavior. Especially at first, the dog will only make the connection between the reward and the behavior if they are immediately joined. As the dog learns how to learn, timing is not as critical and the dog will be able to wait a short time for his reward. To let Louis know he has done well while he is actually

Fig. 7-1. The control point.

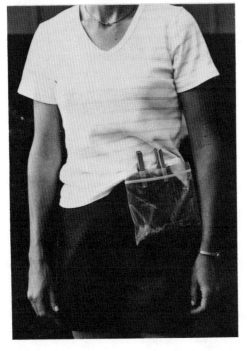

Fig. 7-2. Treats are
immediately accessible.

performing the behavior, give him *quiet* praise, saying, "Go-o-
-od, Louis." Don't excite him with your voice unless he is a
droopy, low-energy type that needs some pumping up. When
you want to release him, do use an excited voice and choose
a release word such as "OK" or "Free" to let him know he can
stop doing whatever you were telling him to do. The release
word can be accompanied by physical petting, depending on
the dog's nature. If Louis is a rough and tumble, good ol' boy,
"OK" can be followed by a few quick pats on the ribs or a
scratch of the ears. If Louis is a quiet, businesslike fellow, gentle
stroking is in order. Keep your petting to a minimum during
training. Your voice and the treat or toy are your chief means
of letting Louis know he is doing well. Your hands should be
reserved for shaping behaviors rather than petting Louis exces-
sively. Use Louis's name before any command in which he must
do something: "Louis, Sit." Do not use his name when you want
him to refrain from doing something: "Stay," not "Louis, Stay."
The dog's name is used as a cue that something is about to
happen that involves him. Try not to use Louis' name as a correction. If you are trying to stop the dog from doing something,
say "No" instead. The dog's name is not a cue word or a word
of correction.

Traditionally, dogs are worked on the handler's left side.
This is a holdover from hunting, when the hunter carried his
gun in his right hand. If it is more convenient for you, feel free
to work the dog on your right side. Just reverse the directions
given in this book as you teach Louis the exercises.

WHICH EXERCISE COMES FIRST?

I recommend you to teach the exercises in the order they
are presented here. In some cases the dog must be performing
one exercise fairly well before he can learn the next one. For
example, the sit is required for the down, recall, and stand for
examination exercises. Louis does not have to be perfect on each
exercise before you introduce another. Give him at least four
or five sessions of training in the sit and sit-stay before you
introduce any other exercise, except for the first part of the recall
as described on page 78. This can be started at any time. Some

dogs can only tolerate a slow rate of training and will become anxious if pushed to learn too much at once. Anxiety makes learning more difficult. Some dogs will breeze through some of the exercises but seem unable to learn others. Reread the training section about the exercise the dog is having difficulty with and be sure you are teaching it properly. If you and Louis are both getting frustrated, stop working on that exercise for a week. You may find a different way to teach the behavior that is more suitable for Louis. Sometimes just the break from stressful training is enough and Louis will suddenly catch on.

OFF-LEASH WORK

The true hallmark of the beginning obedience trainer is a burning urge to get the leash off the dog as soon as possible. Taking a dog off leash too soon can create severe training setbacks, or result in the temporary or permanent loss of the dog. Resist this urge as strongly as you can.

If you choose to work with your dog off leash in an unfenced area, be aware you are taking a calculated risk. The best-trained, most willing dogs can suddenly take a notion to leave and be gone before you can blink. I was working with a Golden Retriever belonging to a young student of mine. I had known the dog for two years and she had lived in my house for a month while I trained her. I was in the process of showing her at the intermediate level in AKC obedience trials. She had won top honors at a recent show and seemed utterly reliable. One evening as we were leaving an obedience class, she was heeling along beside me off-leash as we headed for the car. Suddenly a bunny popped up from nowhere and before I could do anything, dog and bunny were gone. Even a lazy dog can move surprisingly fast. Fortunately, I was able to recover her, but those heart-stopping minutes she was gone taught me a lesson: off-leash work in an open area is always risky. Now you have been warned: make your own decision.

When your dog is ready to work beyond the confines of the six-foot leash, take him to an enclosed area where he cannot run away. Once Louis is letter-perfect in his on-leash work, you may work off-leash indoors.

If you do not have access to an enclosed area, work Louis on a long, light line. This line should be about thirty feet long and may be tied to the dog's collar, or you may buy a clip and tie the line to that. The line should be just strong enough to hold Louis, but not so heavy it acts like an anchor. Put several large knots in the end of the line you will be holding, to have something to grab onto, should Louis make an unexpected exit.

Please remember that no dog is *ever* 100% reliable off-leash, no matter how well trained. There is a real risk any time Louis is not physically attached to you in an unfenced area.

Fig. 7-3. Instinct can overcome even extensive training.

8

The Sit, Watch-Me and Stay

If you are working with a small dog, place him on the table and proceed as outlined below. When he shows you he is making the association between the cue word and the desired behavior, put him on the floor to work the proof-training. As you introduce any new behaviors, put little Louis back on the table to do the initial teaching, then transfer him to ground level.

THE SIT

Face Louis's side with his head to your right and tail to your left. If it is easier for you, you may kneel facing Louis's side. Say "Louis, Sit," in a firm, pleasant voice. Grasp the control point (where the leash and collar join) with your right hand, allowing the rest of the leash to dangle. Slide your left arm under Louis's rump and gently push forward on his knees. At the same time pull backwards on the control point. As Louis's rump nears the ground remove your left hand but maintain pressure on the collar. Hold Louis in the sitting position for three to four seconds, and repeat the cue word, "Sit." *Quietly* praise, "Good boy," as you hold him in position. Then say, "OK" or "Free!" in an excited voice and release the pressure on Louis's collar, allowing him to stand up. Give him a treat immediately. Don't be alarmed if Louis looks at you as though you have lost your mind. This is all very new to him. He will find out in short order that this process means praise, goodies, and exclusive time with Mom or Dad.

An alternate way to teach the sit is with food or a toy (see the photo on page 61). This is especially good for teaching a puppy. With Louis's leash on, hold the control point in your left hand to keep him from moving backward. Show him food or a toy held in your right hand and pass it slowly up and over his nose. Maintain enough pressure on the collar that he cannot lift his front feet off the floor. Give the cue words, "Louis, Sit," in a firm, pleasant voice. Guide his nose upward with the food or toy. As Louis' head comes up, his rump will go down. When his rump touches the floor, repeat the word "Sit," immediately followed by praise, "Good boy," and put the treat or the toy in his mouth. Release him with an "OK" or "Free!" and allow him to stand up. If Louis is very strong or very bouncy, place him with his back in a corner before you start so he cannot back away or squirm too far from you. Repeat this action several times, each time holding the dog in place for a few seconds longer. When Louis will allow you to hold him in place without much squirming for ten seconds, you are ready for the next step.

Fig. 8-1. Step I. Folding the dog into the sit position.

Fig. 8-2. Step II.

Place Louis on your left side and stand up (the toy dog can still be on the table). Grasp the control point with your right hand and fold Louis into a sit, as before. Now straighten, maintaining pressure on Louis's collar to prevent him from getting up. If he gets up anyway, repeat the first steps calmly—Louis still doesn't understand what you want. If Louis lies down, gently pull him back into a sit. If Louis is a very large dog, you will have to get him up and walking before attempting to re-sit him.

Fig. 8-3. Teaching the sit for food.

DOG ATTENTION - THE WATCH-ME

Now that you have some physical control of Louis, you are about to teach him the foundation of all future training: attention. You must have a dog's attention in order to train him. A dog shows he is paying attention by making eye contact with you. You will recall that eye contact is involved in dominance behavior. The alpha figure seeks out eye contact with the subordinate and stares the lower ranking animal into submission. Part of your continued maintenance of the alpha position will be your ability to make and keep eye contact with Louis. This does not mean that you glare menacingly at Louis when you make eye contact. Glaring will force Louis to look away as a gesture of submission to you. Keep a neutral or pleasant expression on your face while teaching the dog to give you eye contact on demand. If Louis is something of a wimp who melts into a puddle of apology whenever you discipline him, keep a soft expression on your face and smile frequently.

Fig. 8-4. *Teaching attention with the dog on the table.*

Now, we have Louis sitting on your left, with your right hand putting gentle pressure on his collar to hold him in place. Transfer the control point to your left hand and maintain the pressure. With your right hand, take hold of Louis' chin and bring his head up and around until you make eye contact. Give the cue words, "Louis, watch me." If Louis fights your holding his chin, you may hold a piece of food in front of his nose and then move it up near your eyes, giving the same cue words. Hold Louis's attention for no more than five seconds, using continuous quiet praise: "Louis, watch me. Go-o-od. Watch me." Release and reward him and repeat the entire procedure. If at any time, Louis gets up or lies down, simply re-sit him and start again. If Louis growls or puts his mouth on you or the leash, administer a scruff-shake and re-sit him without praise or petting until he performs as you wish. Then reward and praise as described above.

When Louis is allowing you to hold his chin without fighting or will turn his head to watch you for the food, you are ready to move on to the next part of this exercise. Remove your hand from his chin, and point to your eyes with no food in your hand, saying, "Louis, watch me." Praise quietly. If he looks away, repeat the cue words and tap him lightly on the nose or on the top of his head with your forefinger, then point to your eyes, repeating the cue words. After five seconds, reward, praise, and release. If you are consistently having problems holding Louis's

Fig. 8-5. Dog attention.

attention for five seconds, go back to using the food or holding his chin. Continue to use the food occasionally even after he will watch you for five seconds without it. You are helping Louis build his attention span slowly, the same as you build endurance for exercise. Until you have had at least two weeks of lessons (more for some dogs), do not expect more than five consecutive seconds of attention without having to remind Louis what you want him to do.

THE STAY

Now we are going to teach Louis to stay in the sit position. With Louis sitting on your left, watching your eyes, continue holding the control point with your left hand. Bring your right hand in front of Louis's face, palm toward his nose, as a signal to stay where he is. Say "Stay" (not "Louis, stay") and step in front of Louis, facing him, with your toes almost touching his toes. Hold him in place with a gentle upward pressure on the control point. Repeat the command word "Stay," and

Fig. 8-6. The Sit-stay. Dog is held in place as the stay signal is given.

prevent Louis from moving by maintaining pressure on the leash. Continue to maintain eye contact either by tapping him on the muzzle with your right forefinger or holding food near your eyes. After five seconds, swing back to where you started, then reward, praise, and release him. Gradually increase the time you hold Louis in the stay position (facing you and paying attention) until he will sit quietly for thirty seconds. Continue to prevent him from making a mistake. If he does manage to break position, re-sit him and start all over again.

If you are working with Louis faithfully and you cannot physically hold him in place after three or four sessions, either because he is too big or too bouncy, and if he is not challenging you for dominance but rather appears not to notice you are trying to train him or communicate with him, it is time to move on to the pinch collar. Be absolutely certain the collar is fitted properly (see p. 31) and proceed *exactly* as outlined above to teach the sit, watch-me and stay. We are not punishing Louis, we are merely having to get a bit more physical to communicate with him. As soon as Louis starts to respond to the training, take the pinch collar away and return to the plain buckle collar. Keep the pinch collar handy, as you may need it again briefly.

Louis is now sitting quietly, allowing you to hold him in place for thirty seconds and giving you attention. Start the sit and stay exercise as usual, holding Louis in place as you swing around to face him. Now relax the pressure on the control point so that the clip of the leash lies loosely on top of Louis's neck. Continue to remind Louis to "Watch" and give him quiet praise. After twenty seconds, again put pressure on the control point to hold Louis in place while you swing back to his side. Reward and release as before. Observe Louis closely while the leash is relaxed and watch for signs that he is going to move. He will probably drop his head, shift his weight, or shuffle his feet before he actually gets up or lies down. If you see these movements, slowly and deliberately (not abruptly) put pressure back on the leash and firmly repeat "Stay" and prevent him from breaking position. Again relax the pressure so that you can see if Louis is beginning to need less help from you to hold his position. If Louis is a toy breed it is now time to put him on the floor, as you will not want to move any distance away from him while he is up on the table.

Fig. 8-7. The Sit-stay. Leash is relaxed slightly so dog remains sitting on his own.

By this time, Louis should be starting to sit by himself when he hears the cue word. If he sits or starts to sit as you reach back to fold his legs under him, he is beginning to make the association between the word "Sit" and the behavior. Now when you tell him to sit, if he does not respond promptly, give a gentle pull upward on the control point to help him.

Gradually increase the time Louis sits facing you with the leash relaxed. As you do so, use a verbal reminder ("Stay") if you see him start to move. If he breaks position, revert to holding him in place a few times. When Louis can hold his sit-stay for sixty seconds, watching you consistently with only a few verbal reminders, eliminate the pressure on the leash as you leave his side and as you return. Louis's sit-stay must be flawless with you standing two inches from his toes before you can move away from him. At this point, we are ready to introduce a few minor distractions. The first few times Louis is presented with distractions, hold him in his sit-stay position with upward pressure on the leash, to prevent him from making a mistake. Expose him to mild distraction for thirty seconds with the leash tight. If he maintains his position and attention, relax the leash and work up to sixty seconds again. Mild distraction means, for example, having another person do something fairly close to

Fig. 8-8. *Ready to administer a sit-stay correction.*

Louis (one of the kids can walk by, rattling paper), but not having anyone call or touch the dog. Or, take Louis to a quiet corner of the park to work. Once Louis has demonstrated to you that he can maintain his position with mild distraction for one minute with you standing toe-to-toe in front of him, it is time to administer mild correction if he breaks. If Louis attempts to

Fig. 8-9. *Introducing minor distraction on the sit-stay. Note handler is ready to administer a correction if necessary.*

get up or lie down, quickly say, "No! Stay!" and tug sharply up on the leash with your hand close to the control point. Use a popping motion, not a pull, and make it last no more than half a second. When he is back in position, give quiet praise. Gradually increase the level of distraction until Louis will hold his stay for one minute under any conditions you can contrive. Be sure to help Louis stay by holding him in place with pressure on the collar each time you introduce a new level of distraction. Now go back to a fairly quiet place and we will begin to move away from Louis and increase the time he must hold his position. Tell Louis to stay, as usual, and then walk to a spot about one foot from Louis and turn to face him. Extend your arm as shown in the illustration and be prepared to administer the mild correction for any movement. Continue to require attention from Louis, reminding him to watch if he begins to look away. During your next few training sessions, increase your distance until you can stand at the end of the leash and Louis will stay steadily for a full minute. Next, increase the time Louis must stay to five minutes.

Fig. 8-10. Sit-stay with major distraction.

If you have a secure place to work, you can now begin off-leash work on the sit-stay. Or, work with the long light line as described on page 43. Start by dropping your end of the leash and letting it lie on the ground between you and the dog. You may want to step on the end of the leash to prevent any unscheduled departures. If Louis proves to be steady in the face of mild distractions, remove the leash entirely and substitute the long light line if working in an open area. Any time Louis breaks position, return him to the spot you left him and repeat the "Stay" cue. If Louis breaks position twice in a row, do a thirty-second stay in the toe-to-toe position, holding him in place with pressure on the collar. If Louis leaves again when you try to work away from him, make your correction more severe. Take hold of Louis's collar (or the control point, if the leash is still attached) and return him rather abruptly to the spot you left him. Repeat "Stay" in a gruff voice and leave him again. If the behavior persists, return Louis to the spot where you left him and give him a scruff-shake before saying "Stay." Any further problems indicate it is time to put the leash back on and retreat several steps in the training process, as Louis either failed to understand what you wanted, or has blanked out on something he previously understood. Continue to build distance from Louis gradually, until he will hold his sit-stay for five minutes while

Fig. 8-11. The sit-stay on the long light line. Note dog attention.

you stand thirty feet away. Add more distractions over a period of several training sessions. Expect Louis to make some mistakes, and reposition him every time he gets up or lies down. Do not yell at him if he starts to move. Repeat "Stay" firmly, return to him and give a gentle upward pop on his collar. Leave him again, but do not go quite as far. Do not be in a big hurry to build distance—be sure the sit-stay is secure with you six feet from Louis before you attempt to move eight feet away.

USES FOR THE SIT-STAY

Place Louis on a sit-stay before he gets into or out of the car. This way, you can control his entrances and exits for his safety and your convenience. Use the sit-stay when answering the front door. Put Louis on a sit-stay between you and the door so he can see who is coming in. This enhances his desire to act as a guard dog, while preventing unauthorized exits or over-exuberant greetings. Keep him on the sit-stay until callers have either left or been greeted and allowed in.

When you introduce Louis to proof-training with guests in your home, I advise you to start with an understanding friend who will not be disturbed or annoyed when you stop the conversation for the sixth time to correct Louis. Wait until Louis is secure in his training before showing off in front of the boss or the new minister. You will be embarrassed if you have to correct Louis in a more formal situation and probably will not do a very good job of it.

When you and Louis are walking together, you (the owner) should go through doors and down stairs first, rather than tripping over each other. Tell Louis to "Sit" and "Stay" until you have the door open and have started through, or until you have started down the stairs. Then release him to follow you. This is especially important if Louis has illusions of being the alpha figure, as the pack leader always goes first.

Any time Louis's exuberance makes him a pest, employ the sit-stay. When you are preparing his dinner (or yours), put him on a sit-stay and free him after you put his dish on the floor or yours on the table. Similarly, when you come home and do

Fig. 8-12. Using the sit-stay as the car door is opened.

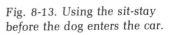

Fig. 8-13. Using the sit-stay before the dog enters the car.

not want to be knocked over or have dirty paw prints added to your outfit, use the sit-stay. Greet Louis quietly and pet him calmly. Then release him when he has settled down a bit.

The Sit Stay at the Front Door

If your dog is one of those that delights in slipping or bolting out the door any time it is opened, use this situation as part of Louis's proof-training. Once Louis can do a reliable sit-stay off leash (or on the long light line) for five minutes, put Louis's leash on and place him on a sit-stay near the door. Have someone else open the door while you quietly correct Louis if he breaks position. If you are working alone you may open the door yourself. First, either tie one end of the leash to a piece of furniture large enough to hold Louis, or put him close enough to the door that you can stand on the end of the leash while you open the door.

Fig. 8-14. Dog on a sit-stay as the door is opened, trainer ready to correct, if necessary.

Some dogs have this bad habit so strongly ingrained that gentle correction makes no impression on them. In that case, escalate to a pain-avoidance correction. This is best done with two people. Get out the pinch collar or the choke chain and put it on Louis. If you are using the choke collar, be sure to put it on properly so that it will indeed choke Louis—otherwise, the point of the correction may be lost. Put Louis's leash on and park him on a sit-stay temptingly near the door. Stand a leash-length away from Louis and be sure you have a firm grip on the leash, but that there is slack between your hands and Louis's collar. Have your accomplice open the door. If Louis does nothing, praise him and release him. Do something else for five minutes, then try again. If he attempts to bolt through the open door, merely stand your ground and hang on to your end of the leash. When Louis hits his end of the leash he will get an unpleasant surprise as the collar causes him pain. If he flies a foot off the ground and hits the floor with a resounding thump, so much the better. During this process, do not jerk or

Fig. 8-15. Let the dog experience the consequences of his behavior.

move the leash and say absolutely nothing. Let Louis do this to and by himself. Now go to him and guide him back to the spot he started from with no praise of any kind. Sit him, repeat "Stay," and leave him again. Go through the entire procedure again. Chances are, Louis will look the other way, as if to say, "Door? What door? I don't see any door." If so praise and release him. Set up this whole scenario at least two more times, preferably a week apart. If Louis is a bright dog, you may need to repeat the sequence using the long light line, so you can be across the room or in another room. Louis must be aware that you can stop him even when the leash is not in evidence.

The Sit for Examination

An important daily use for the sit-stay is to permit you or anyone you designate to touch Louis while he maintains his position. Start by placing Louis on leash, on a sit-stay, while you face him toe-to-toe. Run your hand down Louis's back and do not permit him to move. If he does move, administer a gentle correction and try again. Now handle his legs, feet and tail. When Louis will permit you to do this without breaking his position (he is permitted to wag his tail and give kisses), have someone Louis knows touch him in the same way while you stand ready to reinforce the stay. Next, have someone Louis does not know handle him. This is a preliminary to an exercise we will learn a bit later: the stand for examination. If Louis is an aggressive dog, be prepared to administer a dominance correction if he reacts negatively at any time. If Louis is a shy fellow, this will be a difficult exercise for him. *Be absolutely certain you do not praise, comfort, or reward Louis for acting shy.* Do not pet him or try to reassure him with soothing words when he is afraid. This only rewards the shy behavior and encourages him to continue it. Instead, be matter-of-fact in expecting him to permit another person to touch him. Give a firm "Stay" and hold Louis in place with pressure on the collar, if necessary. It *is* permitted for the *other person* to give Louis a treat before touching him. This will set up a positive association in Louis's mind with being handled. You may only reward Louis *after* he has tolerated the other person's touch and when he obeyed you and stayed.

Most shy dogs will run away when a stranger comes near them. Some, however, will attack if they feel trapped. Such dogs are called *fear-biters* and can be extremely dangerous because they are unpredictable. If Louis appears shy but then snaps when he is approached, do administer a dominance correction and be especially careful not to reward the undesirable behavior. It is essential that fear-biters be neutered and be obedience trained.

Opening the Dog's Mouth — Louis must permit you to open his mouth as part of the examination. Tell Louis to sit and stay. With one hand, gently press Louis's upper lips back against his canine (eye) teeth. With the other, pull down on the front of his lower jaw and hold the jaws apart for a few seconds. Do not open Louis's mouth so wide that he is uncomfortable. Once Louis will permit you to do this without fidgeting or trying to get away, move on to the next step. Open his mouth and continue to hold his upper jaw lightly. Now insert a finger or your entire hand (depending on how big a mouth he has) between his jaws. Hold his upper lip lightly against his teeth so that if he bites down, he will bite his own lip. Now have the other people repeat this procedure. This is the method you will use

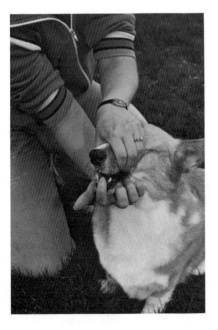

Fig. 8-16. Opening the dog's mouth.

to take things out of Louis's mouth. It is a good idea to practice this with Louis's favorite toy or bone. Take it away and then give it back. If Louis growls or snaps, give him a hard scruff-shake and try again. Now, when you catch Louis with your underwear or the kids' toys, remove them from his mouth and give him his own toy to play with.

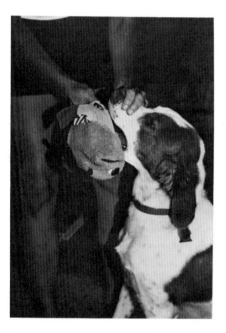

Fig. 8-17. Taking something from the dog's mouth.

QUICK REVIEW

BEHAVIORS: Sit - Watch Me - Stay.

CUE WORDS: Louis, Sit. Louis, Watch Me. Stay.

1. Fold dog into sit, hold in place.
2. Dog attention (watch me)
3. Introduce stay, build time and distance from dog gradually.
4. Dog sits for cue word alone.
5. Sit for examination.
6. Proof-training

9

The Recall

The recall or come when called is the one exercise all dog owners want to teach their pets. There is nothing quite as annoying as a dog that will not come when called, either disappearing over the horizon or dancing enticingly just out of the frantic owner's reach. Before you start to teach this vital behavior to Louis, there are two rules for *you* to learn.

Rule 1: Never chase Louis when he will not come. This merely reinforces his runaway behavior. While he may have left you for some reason which he regards as legitimate (to pursue a passing squirrel), once you start to chase him it becomes a game of tag with you. Unless you are a trained sprinter and Louis is elderly and feeble, there is no way you can catch him. Dogs run faster than almost all people. Turn the tables on Louis—try to get him to chase you. Run away from Louis, preferably laughing loudly (yes, the neighbors will talk about you, but you'll get your dog back). When Louis comes to investigate, wait until he is fairly close then sit or lie down abruptly, ignoring him. When he is within an arm's length, quietly take hold of him. It is also permissible to bribe Louis to come by using food or a toy or the family cat. These tricks will only work a few times and are not a substitute for careful training.

Rule 2: Never punish Louis for coming to you. No matter how angry you are or how long it took to get the little monster back, praise him, reward him, and then confine him. This is one of those times the dog crate (see p. 117) can stop you from committing dogicide. Louis knows from your body posture how angry you are, and it is difficult for him to approach an angry alpha figure. You must praise him with all the enthusiasm you can muster, no matter what you would really like to do to him.

Fig. 9-1. If you can, get the dog to come close by doing something distracting.

Try *not* to use the cue words, "Louis, Come," when you are going to do something less than pleasant to him, like cut his toenails or stuff a pill down his throat. Go and get Louis and bring him where you want him.

There is a difference between teaching a puppy or an average adult dog the recall, and teaching the confirmed runaway to come when called. Let us address the first situation. A puppy should start hearing the words, "Puppy, Come," from the day you bring him home. Call him to play, to eat, or just for a treat. Always squat down as you call, or kneel if you can't squat, to present a less dominating, more welcoming posture. Exuberant praise, treats, and favorite toys should be constant rewards for the puppy who comes when he is called. Encourage the puppy to chase you and reward him when he catches you. In spite of all this early, positive training, there comes a time when Louis the puppy, or Louis the adult, turns a deaf ear to your entreaties and cue words. He will begin to think of lots of things he'd rather do (important sniffing around, for instance) than come when he is called. It will then be time to train him to come whenever he is called, so that he does not believe this is a matter of choice. No dog that will not reliably come when called should ever be allowed off-leash in an unfenced area. The risks are simply too great.

To train the recall, put on Louis's buckle collar and leash and take him to an unfamiliar place. You can start this training the first day along with the sit and stay. Allow him to

Fig. 9-2. The Recall -
Encourage the puppy to
come to you at every
opportunity.

Fig. 9-3. The Recall. Maintain a low profile with a puppy or small dog.

wander ahead of you to the end of the leash as you stroll along. When you are certain Louis's attention is not on you, say "Louis, Come!" in a cheerful voice (not a military drill-sergeant command). Give the leash a quick pop toward you and immediately release the pressure on it, and run *backwards* seven or eight steps. Squat down to greet Louis and reward him with a treat or a toy as he comes to you. You have just invited Louis to chase you and rewarded him for catching you. The quick pop on the collar is not associated with you—you did not correct Louis, as far as he is concerned. Allow Louis to wander off again and repeat the entire sequence. Be sure to squat down and to reward Louis every time he reaches you. When Louis will not take his attention from you long enough to repeat the sequence, you are finished with that exercise for that day. After a few sessions of this, start applying the cue word in the house. Call Louis, run away a few steps and then squat down and reward him when he catches you.

Fig. 9-4. The Recall. Dog wanders at length of leash.

Fig. 9-5 "Louis, come!" Dog is popped toward trainer.

Fig. 9-6. Trainer runs backward as dog runs toward him.

Now we are going to teach Louis to stop and sit in front of you when you call. The purpose of this part of the recall is to be sure he comes *to* you, not gaily romping past you. Do not start teaching this part of the exercise until Louis has had a chance to learn to sit on command, as outlined in Chapter 8. Put Louis on leash and let him drift out ahead of you, even if he keeps an eye on you, anticipating the pop on his collar. Call him and back up as before. If he is not paying attention, use the pop on the collar. If he is, give him the cue words, "Louis, Come," and start backing up without any pressure on the leash. This time, do not squat down, but use the leash to guide him gently to a spot directly in front of you, with his toes almost touching your toes. If Louis is hurrying to you, slowly and calmly reach for the control point as he gets close, letting the rest of the leash dangle. If Louis is stopping to take in the view after taking a few steps toward you, bring him to you with a steady pull, reeling him in hand over hand on the leash until you can reach the control point. Pull up on the control point and say, "Louis, Sit." If he does not sit promptly, reach over his head and tap him gently above the tail, while putting upward pressure on the control point. Now give him a treat, praise

Fig. 9-7. The Recall. Reeling the dog in, hand-over-hand.

and release him. Repeat the sequence several times, until he will sit in front with just light pressure on the control point. Now substitute a treat for the collar pressure. Have the treat in your hand before you call Louis. Call him, back up, say "Louis, sit," and bring the treat up over his nose. As his rump touches the ground, give him the treat, praise and release him. When you call Louis at home now, have him sit in front of you every time. Try to have a treat ready for him every time you call. Should Louis fail to come when you call, go and get hold of his collar and bring him to you, repeating, "Louis, Come."

The second phase of training the recall can be taught as soon as Louis is coming reliably on-leash (off-leash in the house), and sitting in front of you with only a verbal reminder and a treat. You are now going to call Louis from the sit-stay position. This will probably confuse Louis for a few sessions as your previous message to him about the sit-stay has been; "Sit there and don't move until I stand next to you and release you." Now that message is going to change to; "Sit there until I either tell you to do something else *or* return to your side and release you." To minimize this confusion, I substitute the cue

Fig. 9-8. The Recall. Helping the dog sit in front of you.

word "Wait" for "Stay" when I am going to call my dog or send him to retrieve or jump in advanced training. "Wait" tells the dog, "I *am* going to tell you to leave the sit position and do something else." You may make this substitution if you wish, but it is not necessary. Louis can easily learn that "Stay" has an additional meaning.

Put Louis on leash and tell him to sit and stay (or wait). Go to the end of the leash and face Louis. Show him the treat or the toy and say, "Louis, Come!" in an excited voice. Give a gentle pop on the leash to start him moving toward you, and run backwards away from him about ten steps. Guide him to you with the leash and use the treat to help him sit in front of you. Praise Louis enthusiastically and release him. If Louis runs past you before you can guide him into a sit in front of you, just turn around and continue to backpedal in the opposite direction and guide him to a sit in front of you. The second or third time you repeat this part of the recall, Louis will probably anticipate your action and start to come before you call him. This merely indicates he is confused about the new variation on the sit-stay. Quietly take him back to the place he was left, remem-

Fig. 9-9. The sit in front for food (in trainer's hand).

bering that Louis is never punished when he comes to you. Re-sit him and start again. You may have to give him a verbal reminder to stay, but do not administer any physical correction. Be patient until he can figure out the new rules. Once this has been accomplished, get out the long light line and attach it to Louis's collar. Start increasing your distance from Louis before you call him, taking several sessions to get to the end of the line twenty to thirty feet away from the dog. Reel in the line, hand over hand, letting your end dangle or lie on the ground as Louis gets closer to you. Keep the training as positive as possible. Continue to run backwards as you call Louis. When Louis is coming to you nicely the full distance of the line, reduce your backpedaling to one step backwards. This will be an ongoing physical cue to Louis to reinforce the "come" cue word. At this time you may begin gradually reducing the number of times Louis receives his treat or toy when he comes to you. Do not, however, eliminate the reward entirely. Continue to produce a goodie at least once every training session no matter how advanced Louis is in his training. *Always* praise Louis when he comes to you.

Now, introduce some proof-training to the recall lessons. As before, start with something only mildly distracting and work your way up to whatever is hardest for Louis to resist—a cat walking by, the kids playing ball or Frisbee, or the corner hot dog vendor. Have somebody wave a treat under Louis's nose just when you call him. If Louis fails to start towards you when he hears the cue words, a pop on the leash or long light line will compel him in your direction. Similarly, if he starts toward you but then veers off toward the distraction you have carefully arranged, pop him toward you and repeat, "Louis, Come!" Praise and reward him when he gets to you.

When Louis is letter-perfect on the recall in any situation you can create, you may remove the leash and/or line. Any failure to respond means a session on leash or on the line is in order. Think carefully before you take Louis off-leash in an unfenced area. If he has a strong hunting instinct and flushes a bird, squirrel, or bunny in the park or in a field, all of his training may simply fall out of his head. This is more than simple disobedience. It takes a great deal of time and effort, and usually some pain avoidance work to overcome an instinctive

Fig. 9-10. The recall on leash with major distraction.

behavior. I have trained several dogs from breeds originally pro-
duced to herd livestock. In at least three cases these dogs had
advanced obedience titles and were well aware of the meaning
of "Come." The first few times these dogs saw sheep, their
instinct to chase and circle was so powerful that no commands
I gave made the slightest impression. It took a great deal of additional training to overcome the power of that natural instinct
and re-establish verbal control of these dogs when sheep or cattle
were present.

TRAINING THE RUNAWAY

For the chronic runaway, we will use the first part of the
training sequence described above, with a few variations.
Remember that the chronic runaway did not develop the
behavioral problem overnight, and you are not going to solve
it quickly. There is no element of surprise to this training. It
will start as mild pain avoidance, using the buckle collar. If you
cannot move Louis with the buckle collar, or if he continues
to try to bolt at every opportunity after a few sessions of recall
training, escalate to the pinch collar, or even to the choke chain.
This training cannot begin until Louis has accomplished a solid
five-minute sit-stay on leash, of course. Put Louis on a sit-stay
and go to the end of the leash. Turn and face him and say,
"Louis, Come," in a cheerful voice, giving a hard enough pop
on the leash to get Louis up and moving toward you. Run backwards several steps and continue to pop the leash and repeat
the cue words. When Louis reaches you, squat down to receive

him and reward and praise him. Continue this exercise in this manner until Louis is getting up and hustling toward you as soon as the word "Come" is spoken, and preferably before you can pop him with the leash. At this point, introduce the sit in front as described previously. Do use reward and praise, and do try to make this a positive experience for Louis. Make it clear, however, that he has no choice in the matter.

Next, progress to long line work and *stay with it at least twice as long as you think you should.* Call Louis when you are in the house and if he fails to come, go get him. If he starts to play catch-me games in the house, run away from him or sit down and ignore him pointedly until he comes to investigate why you are not chasing him. Do not chase or yell at him. Calmly take hold of him and put his leash on. Do several on-leash recalls with no treats or rewards. Do praise him. Let him wear the leash at all times around the house for several days, until he is responding to your command to come every time.

When Louis is totally reliable on the long line off-leash in the house, proceed with proof-training, again, staying with it for at least several weeks after he has begun to respond reliably. Next, let Louis trail the leash or line from his collar and work in a larger enclosed area. If Louis fails to come at any time, step on the end of the leash or line and reel him in rather abruptly. Do some work on-leash and then try again. Don't rush into any off-leash work, even in the enclosed area, if it is too large for you to catch him promptly.

QUICK REVIEW

Behaviors: The Recall

Cue Words: Louis, Come. Louis, Sit.

1. Wait until dog is distracted, run backwards, guide him to you.
2. Have dog sit in front of you when he reaches you.
3. Recall from the sit-stay, gradually increasing distance from dog.
4. Proof-train.

10

The Down
and Stay

When a dog lies down, he makes himself vulnerable to attack. When you make Louis lie down, you are physically asserting your dominance over him, no matter how gently you work with him. For these reasons, the down position can be a tough one for many dogs to learn. Teaching Louis to lie down on command is most likely to bring up dominance issues and provoke a struggle for alpha position. Be very cautious in teaching this exercise if Louis has already contended with you for pack leadership. If there are other dogs around when you do your training, trouble is more likely to occur because Louis feels himself to be vulnerable to these dogs. On the other hand, an extended down-stay is one of the safest, least stressful ways to settle a dominance issue in your favor.

This training can begin when Louis has a good grasp of sit and stay, with you standing toe-to-toe in front of him, leash relaxed. Put Louis's leash on and have him sit on your left. Kneel down next to him. If Louis is rambunctious, kneel on the leash, or wrap it around your leg. Run your left hand up and down Louis's back a few times, and then reach over his shoulder and take hold of his left ankle with your left hand. If you can't reach, refer to the variation for giant breeds below. Now put your right hand on Louis's right ankle. If Louis becomes nervous when you hold his ankles, spend one or two sessions going only this far. Next, lift Louis's legs, one at a time, until his paws hang limply, showing he is relaxed (see fig. 10-1). Take hold of both of Louis's ankles and slide them forward, while simultaneously using your left elbow to press Louis against your body and to put him off balance. Use the cue words, "Louis, Down," and slide Louis's ankles forward until his elbows rest on the floor. Your left elbow will be across Louis's back, gently pressing him to the ground. Stay absolutely calm during this process.

Fig. 10-2. The Down. Dog's feet are relaxed.

Fig. 10-2. The Down. Dog is gently lowered to the ground. Trainer's left elbow presses dog toward her body.

If Louis struggles with you, but doesn't growl or snap, you may have to hold him down with your upper body instead of just your elbow. While inelegant, this is effective. Keep your right hand on Louis's ankle and stroke Louis's back with your left hand, using long, slow strokes, gently maintaining a downward pressure to reinforce the position. Repeat "Louis, Down. Go-o-od boy," quietly several times as you stroke his back. After fifteen seconds, release and reward him. Repeat the procedure several times, until he will lie quietly while you hold him in place for fifteen seconds. If at any time Louis growls or snaps, immediately use the scruff-shake and then proceed with training. Do not allow Louis to put his mouth on your hands or arms at any time during this procedure, as this may be a prelude to an argument about dominance. Say, "No!" sharply and if he continues to mouth your anatomy, administer a scruff-shake.

You can also teach Louis to lie down for food. This can be effective with puppies and large dogs. Place Louis in a sit and kneel beside him, as in the previous method. Put your left hand on top of Louis's shoulders and hold a piece of food in

Fig. 10-3. *Sometimes it is necessary to use sheer body weight to hold the dog down. Photo by Kent Dannen.*

your right hand. Put the food in front of his nose, and say, "Louis, Down." Draw the food slowly forward and down, while lightly pressing down on Louis's shoulders. As his elbows touch the ground, give him the food and stroke his back as in the other method. If Louis crawls forward, restrain him with the leash. If only his front end goes down, rest your forearm along his spine and push down along the entire length of his back.

Fig. 10-4. The Down for food. Step I. Focusing the dog on the food.

Fig. 10-5. Step II. Drawing the food toward the ground.

For the extremely large dog, we will alter the method somewhat. Have Louis sit, and kneel down facing him. Handle each of Louis's legs separately as described above, until his paws hang limply, but from the front rather than the side. When Louis seems relaxed, grasp both of his front legs just below the elbows. Say, "Louis, Down," and pull forward until Louis's elbows are on the ground. Maintain downward pressure on Louis's forelegs for fifteen seconds, then praise, reward and release him.

Fig. 10-6. The Down for a large dog. Step I. Grasp the dog's legs just below the elbow.

When Louis is able to relax and lie still for fifteen seconds with you holding him in position, tell him, "Stay," give the hand signal (palm facing the dog's nose) and let go. Insist now that Louis watch you while he lies down where you left him. When he will lie still for fifteen seconds without you having to touch him, try standing up, at his side, holding the leash in your hand. If he starts to get up, repeat "Stay" in a firm voice. If he succeeds in getting up, start all over again. You may need to stay on the ground with him for a longer period. Remember, this is a difficult position for some dogs. While he is down, Louis should be fairly still. He may lie on his chest, his side, or even on his back, (there are always some clowns who prefer this) but he should not shift back and forth more than once. Too much shifting means he is planning to get up, or at least is fighting the intent of the down-stay. Once Louis will lie still for one minute with you at his side, stand in front of him in the toe-to-toe position for a few sessions. When he is handling this well, begin to build time and distance as in the sit-stay. If Louis gets up consistently, go back to holding him in place for several sessions.

Fig. 10-7. Step II. Pull the legs forward.

Fig. 10-8. Step III. Use downward pressure to hold the dog in place.

When Louis is starting to lie down before you can put him down, it is time to teach him to lie down with just the cue word and a gesture toward the floor. Have Louis sitting on your left and grasp the control point with your left hand. Say, "Louis, Down," lock your elbow and push your left hand to the floor. If you have done your preliminary work well, Louis should offer little resistance. If he does, there are several options. The first is to accompany your cue word with a piece of food held in your right hand and drawn toward the floor as you press down on the control point with your left hand. Or, face Louis in the toe-to-toe position. Stand or kneel on the leash, depending on Louis's size. Bend over and grasp his right leg above the elbow with your right hand. With your left hand, push sideways (to the right) firmly on Louis's left shoulder as you pull his right leg forward. This will throw Louis off balance and he will more or less fall over. The final method is a form of mild pain avoidance and should only be used if Louis is NOT resisting the original training in which you gently pulled his legs forward and if the other methods do not produce the desired results. If he is still resisting the original training, he is not ready for the down with just a verbal command. Stand next to Louis as you would for a sit-stay. Hold the handle end of the leash in your right hand. This is easier to teach if you wear leather soled shoes with a heel, rather than rubber-soled shoes, so that the leash can slide freely under your foot. Place your left foot on top of the middle of the leash so that the leash is under your instep. Give the cue words, "Louis, Down," and pull steadily upward on the leash. You may need to use both hands. Louis's head will be drawn downward by the pressure on the collar. If Louis only puts his neck on the floor, but leaves his rump in the air, calmly and quietly repeat, "Down," as you maintain pressure upwards on the leash. I have seen dogs stubbornly maintain this awkward position for as long as three minutes. Stay calm and keep the pressure on. Louis will eventually put the rest of his body on the floor. When he does; praise, reward and release. Repeat the exercise, and note that it takes far less time for Louis to lie down the second time (rump included) than it did the first time. Eventually, Louis will lie down with only the cue word and a slight upward pull on the leash.

Now switch back to the first method I described—pushing downward on the control point—to make Louis lie down. When you find that Louis is lying down before you can put any pressure on the control point, stop helping him with the leash and limit yourself to a verbal cue and pointing to the ground. At this time, if Louis ignores the command to lie down, you may administer a mild correction. This is done by seizing the control point and pushing your hand to the floor in an abrupt manner. Correct Louis in this way for breaking the down-stay as well.

Use the long light line and work until Louis will stay for five minutes with you thirty feet away. It is not necessary that Louis maintain eye contact with you for the full five minutes. He should, however, respond immediately to the cue words "Watch me." If he does not, go to him and tap him on the muzzle with your forefinger, repeating, "Louis, Watch me." You should be able to call for and get Louis's attention at any time. Proceed with proof-training as you did in the sit-stay.

Fig. 10-9. Forcing the dog to lie down. Lock your elbow and push down on the control point.

Fig. 10-10. Lift one foot and press on the opposite shoulder, while giving the cue word, "Louis, Down."

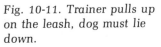

Fig. 10-11. Trainer pulls up on the leash, dog must lie down.

USES FOR THE DOWN-STAY

Remember that your ability to make Louis lie down and stay is an important reminder to him that you are the alpha figure. One of the best uses for the down-stay is to reinforce that message. Once Louis will stay for five minutes during training, you may proceed to use the long down at home. Put on Louis's collar and leash. Place him on a down-stay next to your favorite chair. No one else should be in the room and there should be no distractions at this time. If Louis is a rambunctious dog, tie him to the chair or your leg with the leash. Otherwise, let the leash dangle. Sit back and read a book or watch TV. Keep an eye on Louis. If he falls asleep next to your chair, terrific. If he breaks position as soon as he sees you pick up your book, give him a collar correction as described above and return him to the spot where he was left. Be very sure that this correction is calm and deliberate, not angry and excited. We are trying to keep Louis quiet, not rev him up. After ten minutes, reward, praise and release. Let Louis walk around for a few minutes, then repeat the ten minute down-stay. Over the next week, work up to a thirty minute down-stay, calmly and slowly correcting Louis any time he breaks position. Obviously, Louis may need to shift position more than once during a thirty-minute period. Just be sure shifting does not become getting up and leaving. Now introduce distractions. Bring Louis in when the family is watching TV and eating popcorn, and have him lie next to you through an entire half-hour program. Use the thirty minute down-stay in the kitchen while you prepare dinner. Tie Louis's leash to the kitchen table or to the refrigerator, or some other secure place which will serve to anchor him safely. Proceed with your work, watching Louis out of the corner of your eye. Correct him if he gets up. When Louis will hold his position reliably, take the leash off. Put Louis across the room from you, preferably in a corner so he will be out of the way and will not feel exposed to the world.

Use this training when guests come. Allow Louis to greet the guests, if he is not too rowdy. If he is, use the sit-stay. Then put him in his corner so he can enjoy being part of the household activities without making a nuisance of himself, or frightening or annoying guests who are not fond of dogs. Put Louis on a down-stay in the corner while the family eats dinner. No begging allowed! Also, no whining or pitiful moaning. Louis can enjoy your company (and you, his) from a distance of ten feet. He does not have to have his nose in your plate to be your companion. Now you can find out if the kids have actually been eating their liver or if Louis has been the under-the-table recipient all along. In addition to these benefits, regular thirty-minute down-stays remind the dog that you are the boss and go a long way toward resolving dominance struggles. Remember not to try this for the first time when your guests are not well known to you. Either you will be uncomfortable in having to correct Louis or you will fail to correct him at all, which can set you back considerably in your training.

Fig. 10-12. The long down in the kitchen. Louis can enjoy your company without being underfoot.

If you do not use the dog crate (see p. 120) to confine Louis in the car, do use the down-stay. The ideal place for Louis to ride in the car is on the floor of the back seat. If you usually drive alone, however, Louis can ride on the floor in front of the passenger seat. If you have a station wagon, give Louis the spot between the back seat and the back window. The first few times you use the down-stay in the car, have someone else drive so you can control Louis. If Louis is accustomed to sitting on the driver's lap or rocketing back and forth over the seats, it may take a while for him to understand that the rules have changed. Be persistent—it is important for his safety and yours.

QUICK REVIEW

Behavior: Down and Stay

Cue Words: Louis, down. Stay.

1. Dog allows ankles to be held, trainer's arm over dog's shoulder.
2. Dog gently lowered to ground and held in place.
3. Introduce stay, build time and distance gradually.
4. Dog lies down for cue word alone.
5. Proof-training.

11

The Stand
and Stay
for Examination

I n teaching Louis this exercise, you will win the undying gratitude of your veterinarian, and your groomer, if you use one. To teach the stand, have Louis sit. Kneel down, facing his side, in the same way you started to teach the sit. Put your right hand under Louis's chin, palm down, and take hold of his collar so your knuckles touch his throat. Say, "Louis, Stand," and gently pull straight forward (not up or down) on the collar. Do this slowly and deliberately, not abruptly. As Louis's weight shifts forward, put your left hand on the inside of Louis's right thigh (just above his knee joint) and very gently press backwards (toward Louis's tail). As Louis assumes the stand position, hold him in place for a few seconds, then lightly stroke his thigh or his belly with your left hand. Then praise, reward and release. Repeat the exercise until Louis is standing with only the pressure on his collar. Continue to stroke him with your left hand while he is standing. Maintain gentle pressure on the collar and repeat "Louis, Stand" several times as you stroke Louis's back, legs, feet and tail. This will not be new to him, as you have already taught him to accept your touch anywhere on his body during the sit for examination. If Louis starts to sit while you are stroking him, gently press backwards on his thigh and repeat, "Stand." If he manages to sit, or walks away, start all over again. When Louis will stand quietly for fifteen seconds while you hold his collar, add the "Stay" cue word and hand signal, and try standing up, still holding the collar lightly. If Louis moves about, pull forward on the collar and repeat, "Stand, Stay."

When Louis appears steady, swing around to face Louis in the toe-to-toe position. Hold the collar lightly or hold his chin in your hand to remind him to stay. Run your free hand down his back and handle his feet as before. Now use both hands to open his mouth as in the sit for examination. Have other people examine Louis. If Louis is very bouncy and exuberant, continue to hold his collar or head lightly as the other people examine him. If he sits while being examined, either bend over and touch his thigh, or if you can't reach that far, swing back around beside him and reposition him. Work with Louis until he will stand quietly for thirty seconds while someone handles him. If Louis is shy you may never be able to let go of him while he is being handled by a stranger. Do insist that he stay standing, even if you have to hold him in place. You might try having anyone who comes up to handle Louis give him a treat first. If Louis thinks food is associated with allowing himself to be touched, he may become more accepting. When Louis is comfortable standing for examination and will hold his position for thirty seconds, try the exercise without holding him in any way. Stay close enough that you can give him a mild collar correction (a forward pull on the collar and a firm "Stay") if he moves away.

Fig. 11-1. Pulling the dog up into the stand position — note position of trainer's hands.

Fig. 11-2. Holding the dog in the stand position and getting a kiss in the process.

USES FOR THE STAND FOR EXAMINATION

As mentioned previously, this exercise is wonderful for use in the veterinarian's office. Stand Louis on the examining table and hold him lightly from the front or the side, depending on what part the vet is examining.

Have Louis stand and stay for grooming and/or bathing. If Louis is extremely hairy and brushing him is a marathon exercise, have him lie down for most of it. Then use the stand-stay to work on parts you could not reach while he was lying down. Most dogs enjoy being brushed, although it may take them a while to realize that they like it. Keep treats coming throughout a grooming session to make the experience more pleasurable.

When Louis has been romping in the mud, put him on a stand-stay at the door and wipe his feet before he can track the back yard in and grind it into your carpeting. If Louis is a short-haired dog that must wear a sweater when he goes out in the cold, have him stand and stay while you dress him.

Fig. 11-3. Teaching the stand on the table.

Fig. 11-4. Hold the dog in place while another person handles him.

QUICK REVIEW

Behavior: The Stand and Stay for Examination

Cue Words: Louis, Stand. Stay.

1. Guide dog into standing position and hold him there.
2. Introduce stay and add examination by owner.
3. Examination by stranger, owner holding dog's collar.
4. Owner moves away, stranger examines dog.

12

Walking
on Leash

T here are two ways to teach a dog to walk on leash. The first—the "don't pull"—is sufficient for walking with the dog in uncrowded areas or for jogging with the dog on leash. The second way—heeling—is used for walking a dog on crowded city streets. The point of both types of on-leash walking is that Louis does not pull you down the street, run between your legs, or otherwise interfere with your forward progress. If you are sure you will never be walking Louis on crowded streets, it is not necessary to teach him to heel. The don't pull will be sufficient.

THE DON'T PULL

The idea of this exercise is that Louis walk on your left, staying within the range permitted by the leash, without at any time pulling or dragging you. If you have been allowing Louis to drag you for any period of time when you walk together, this is going to be a bit more difficult than if Louis has rarely walked on a leash. If Louis has worn a choke chain when he dragged you along, it will be even more difficult. He will have built up an immunity to the pain and choking action of the collar. Immediately switch him to a correctly-fitted pinch collar and follow the steps outlined below. Once Louis learns to walk comfortably with you, switch back to the buckle collar.

Put on Louis's buckle collar and leash. Have your food reward ready. Take Louis to a fairly quiet place. Start by having him sit on your left and watch you. If you have been working on the recall, chances are Louis will keep an eye on you

Fig. 12-1. The difference between heeling and the
don't-pull position. The dog in front is
demonstrating the don't-pull — note the slack in
the leash. The black and white dog is heeling —
note the attention he is paying to the hander.

as you walk forward. Start walking at a brisk pace. Guide Louis
with the leash to your left (or right, if you prefer, but be consistent). Allow Louis to drift (or charge) to the end of the leash.
When the leash tightens, say "Don't pull," and give a quick
pop on the leash to stop his forward motion. Reach forward and
give him a treat, praise him and walk on. The point is that there
be slack in the leash, even if it is only for a moment. Do not
pop Louis so hard his feet leave the ground. If Louis is pulling
ahead of you or to your side, pop toward your body as you say,
"Don't pull." The pop only needs to be hard enough to check
Louis's momentum and remind him he is attached to you. If
Louis falls behind you, do not drag him. Turn around, squat
down and coax him to catch up, using the food to help him
come toward you. When he catches up, turn back and walk on
at a brisk pace. If Louis is a large dog and you cannot check
his forward motion with just your arms, get a good grip on the
leash and stop, setting your entire body weight against him.
Let Louis hit the end of the leash and say, "Louis, don't pull."
When there is slack in the leash even for a moment, walk on.
If you still can't stop him, go home and get the pinch collar

and proceed as outlined above. If you are jogging or walking for exercise with Louis, let him empty himself before you start and then keep him moving along. If the purpose of the walk is for him to eliminate, let Louis set the pace and stop when he wants to stop. Do not allow Louis to urinate or defecate on anyone else's lawn or shrubs. Carry a plastic bag with you and pick up any droppings. Put the bag over your hand, pick up the offending matter and close the bag. Toss it into the nearest trash receptacle or take it home with you and dispose of it. Part of having a dog is being responsible for cleaning up after the animal. Please do not become one of those undesirable neighbors who keeps his own yard clean by allowing his dog to dirty the neighbors' yards or the public park.

Fig. 12-2. Walking with Louis in the "don't pull" position.

Continue to work with Louis on the don't pull, increasing the amount of distraction gradually. Reach forward and give Louis a treat every time you see him correct himself when he begins to feel pressure on his collar or realizes he has reached the end of the leash. Say. "Go-o-od Louis," every time you reward him. Repeat the cue words and give a pop on the leash *every time* Louis allows the leash to tighten. He will soon get the message that he can wander around on your left side, but it is his responsibility to keep slack in the leash. Louis will learn exactly how far he can wander. This is one time I am going to suggest a timetable for an exercise. If you are training Louis regularly or jogging or walking with him at least five days per week, by the end of two weeks, it is reasonable to expect that he will not need more than one or at most two reminders not to hit the end of the leash during a session. If he needs frequent commands and pops on the leash, it is time to escalate to the pinch collar. As soon as Louis gets the message, go back to the buckle collar.

If you are walking on sidewalks, you will want Louis to stop when you come to a curb. If Louis is walking ahead of you at the end of the leash, without pulling, he will reach the curb before you do. As he does, give a steady but gentle pull on the leash and say "Louis, Stop." Maintain pressure on the leash as you take a step or two to catch up with Louis. When you reach his side, praise, reward, and (if no cars are coming), say, "OK!-Louis, Don't Pull," and walk on. Repeat this sequence until Louis begins to stop at the curb by himself before you can check him with the leash. Now drop the "stop" cue word, but continue to praise him every time he stops at a curb. If he gets sloppy about this, and starts stepping into the street before you reach his side, go back to stopping him with the leash and the cue word for several sessions.

If Louis is an aggressive dog, or if other dogs are frequently running loose in the area where you train or exercise, think twice before letting Louis off the leash, no matter how well he is responding to the training. If a stray dog comes near you, stamp your feet and yell "Go home!" This will keep most dogs away. If the stray dog persists, pick up a few small stones or a handful of gravel. Wave your arms, yell "Go home!" and throw the gravel on the ground in front of the dog. Do not

Fig. 12-3. Stopping at the curb.

attempt to hurt the dog: it is not his fault he has an irresponsible owner who allows him to run at large.

When Louis is consistently walking without any pulling, you may choose to allow him off leash, but *never on city streets or where there is traffic*. The dangers of Louis causing an accident or being hurt are too great. If you are walking in a park or on back country roads, and *only* if Louis is reliable on the recall, you may remove the leash. Do it for short periods at first and call Louis back to you frequently for praise and reward. Then put the leash back on and continue on your way. As Louis proves himself trustworthy, extend the time he is allowed off leash. When I walk on the country roads with my dogs, I imagine an invisible leash about fifty feet long. Any time my dog goes beyond that limit, I call his name and say, "That's far enough." My dogs have all learned that this means they are not to go any farther. They will either stop and wait for me to catch up or come back to me. You must read your own dog, however, and use your judgment. With all the training my dogs have received I have still been unable to prevent several aromatic encounters with skunks that were strolling along the side of the road. Tomato juice, by the way, followed by several soapings, is effective in de-skunking a dog as long as you don't plan to get very close to him for a few days.

Uses for the Don't Pull

Obviously you will use this behavior any time Louis is walking with you on leash. Combine the don't pull with the other exercises Louis has learned. As you and Louis are strolling along, stop briefly and leave him on a sit-stay. Let the leash hang from his collar. Walk on for some distance, then turn and call him to come. If you stop to chat with someone while you are walking, have Louis do a sit-stay or a down-stay until you are finished.

QUICK REVIEW

Behavior: The Don't Pull

Cue Words: Louis, Don't pull. Louis, Stop.

1. Dog is checked every time he allows the leash to tighten.
2. Dog stops at the curb, first with help and then by himself.
3. Proof-training.
4. Off-leash work, if applicable and if recall is reliable.

HEELING ON LEASH

A dog in the heel position stays close to your left leg at all times. His neck is approximately even with your leg and he does not leave heel position to bolt ahead or dart between your legs. Louis can learn both heeling and the don't pull. You may teach either one first, but do not introduce the new instruction until he is fairly secure in the first one taught. I prefer to start with the don't pull, which is less difficult for the dog to learn as it does not require as much precision and concentration as heeling. There is a special technique we will use for dogs shorter than twelve inches at the shoulder. The information that follows is for dogs taller than twelve inches.

To teach Louis to heel, sit him on your left and get his attention. Take all the slack out of the leash by gathering it in your left hand. There should be enough pressure on Louis's collar to hold him in the heel position next to your leg. Keep your left hand (with the folded up leash) at waist level and have several treats ready in your right hand. Say, "Louis, Heel," and walk forward briskly so Louis is trotting. Hold Louis securely in position next to your leg by maintaining pressure on the leash. If Louis has been dragging you around town for any length of time or if he is so big you cannot hold him in place with one hand, you would be better off to teach him the don't pull before you teach him to heel. Then he will understand that he must think about where he is walking while on leash, before you try to teach him to maintain an exact position next to your leg. Reach across your body with your right hand and keep feeding Louis small pieces of treats or squeaking the toy as you walk. If Louis continuously leaps up to try to get the food, you must administer a mild correction. Say, "No!" and pop on the leash to force him down. A leaping dog is not learning. He must wait for the treat until you hand it to him. Insist that he watch you throughout the exercise. The first time you attempt to teach Louis to heel, walk in a straight line for some twenty to thirty steps, holding Louis next to your leg with your left hand and feeding him every three or four steps with your right hand.

Fig. 12-4. Heeling on a loose leash, with excellent dog attention.

Continue to hold Louis in the heel position, using frequent rewards, until he can walk a block without trying to leave your side. Now, gradually loosen the pressure on the collar to allow Louis to maintain heel position (his neck next to your left leg) by himself. Keep the treats coming and keep his attention by repeating, "Louis, watch me," any time he looks away. If Louis drifts away, gently and deliberately tighten the leash again to show him what you want, repeating, "Louis, Heel. Go-o-od boy." Do not jerk on the leash. When Louis can walk a full block with the leash relaxed, with frequent treats, he is beginning to understand the meaning of the word "heel." Begin to withdraw the treats, only giving them occasionally. Keep the praise coming. At this point, if he leaves heel position, you may administer a mild correction by making a quick pop on the leash toward your left leg, repeating the cue words. Add a stop and stand or sit about every ten paces. Be sure to stop and have Louis stand or sit at every curb, so that he learns not to dart out into traffic.

Whenever you stop, Louis should stop. In traditional obedience training, dogs are taught to sit automatically in the heel position when the trainer stops. This is an optional behavior. You may choose to allow Louis simply to stop and stand next to you when you come to a halt. To accomplish this, give the cue words, "Louis, Stop," as you come to a halt. Restrain Louis by holding him in place with the leash. If Louis chooses to sit (some dogs do), fine. If not, all we want is that he cease to move forward until he is again told to heel. Hold Louis in place for a few seconds, praise, and then repeat, "Louis, Heel," and walk on. As Louis begins to stop by himself when you come to a halt, stop holding him in position next to your leg and just use the cue words, "Louis, Stop," to remind him to halt when you do. If you are doing a lot of heeling with Louis, (on daily walks, for example) you may eventually drop the cue words and expect Louis to stand quietly next to your leg any time you stop walking. If he forgets and wanders past you, give him a pop on the collar and repeat the cue words a few times to refresh his memory.

If you want Louis to sit every time you stop, proceed as described below. Having him sit does reinforce for the dog the idea that forward motion has ceased and that he must wait to

Fig. 12-5. *Louis may learn to sit everytime you stop, but it is not necessary.*

move on again until you are ready. If Louis has already learned to sit on command, say, "Louis, Sit," and come to a stop. Reward, praise and release. If Louis still needs help to sit, you will need a bit of coordination to assist him. Try what I am about to describe without the dog a few times or you will confuse Louis. Several steps before you intend to stop, reach across your body and take hold of the control point with your right hand. Try to have no food in your hand as you do this. If you do have food, it won't prevent you from grasping the control point, but it may make the leash a little sticky. Say, "Louis, sit," and reach back with your left hand to fold Louis's rear under as you gently pull backward on the control point. Reward, praise and release. Continue to fold Louis into a sit as you teach heeling, until he begins to sit before you can reach his rear. Then, just use the cue word "sit," and the pressure on the collar to make him sit every time you stop. When you are ready to move forward again, get Louis's attention, say "Louis, Heel," and start moving.

Louis is now ready for some proof-training. Gradually increase the level of distraction, remembering to hold him in place with the leash to prevent mistakes the first few times you expose him to a new situation. Continue to withdraw the food rewards, so that Louis only gets an occasional treat. Keep praising him.

When Louis can walk on a city sidewalk (if you don't ever walk him on city sidewalks, he really doesn't need to learn to heel) with the leash relaxed, paying attention to you, and sitting when you stop, try changing your pace. Take long slow steps and prevent him from forging ahead. Break into a run or a fast trot and keep him in heel position. Make some fast turns or circles. Heel him on different surfaces—grass, dirt, concrete, etc. Even when he is performing to your satisfaction under any circumstances you can devise, I would still advise you not to take Louis off leash around traffic. If you are in a situation in which you need to use heeling rather than the don't pull, Louis should be on leash.

Heeling With A Small Dog

If you are working with a small dog and want him to sit when you stop walking, be sure he will sit on command before starting the heeling training. Work with him on the table first, and then on the ground. By the time you begin teaching the heeling, he must sit with only the cue word and slight pressure on the collar. We are basically going to use the same technique, but a change of equipment is in order. We are going to make a solid leash. The solid leash was originally used in Europe to train dogs that were dangerously aggressive. It could be used to force the dog to keep some distance from the trainer so the dog could learn but couldn't bite. Now we will use it with little dogs and for people with back problems which make bending over difficult. It can be used for larger dogs, but you must shorten the length of the dowel accordingly.

To make a solid leash, go to the lumber yard or hardware store and buy a piece of wooden dowel rod long enough to reach from your hip to a point even with the dog's neck when he is sitting in the heel position. The dowel should be rather light, generally no more than half an inch in diameter. Also buy a leash clip, either at an Army surplus store or a horse supply store. The clip should be as small as possible. Drill a hole through one end of the dowel, one inch from the end. With string or fine wire, attach the leash clip to the dowel through the hole you have drilled, leaving at least three inches of cord between the dowel and the snap. You may now proceed as out-

Fig. 12-6. Teaching heeling with the solid leash. The dog is being held in heel position and is giving the trainer good eye contact. Gradually, you will allow some slack between the collar and the dowel.

lined for the larger dogs, using the cord between the end of the dowel and the leash clip to provide slack when Louis is ready to heel without your help. If you cannot bend, use a squeaky toy rather than food to keep Louis's attention. Tie a light piece of string to the toy so you can retrieve it without bending. Let him play with the toy for a few seconds after he sits when you stop. Once Louis is heeling reliably with no pressure on his collar, you may switch back to your regular leash for his daily walks.

It is possible to teach a toy dog (or any dog) to catch food on the fly. Start tossing small pieces to him while he sits in your lap or on the table. If he misses frequently, drop the food on his head, hitting him between the eyes, until he begins to catch it regularly. Gradually increase the length of your throw. Never let him pick the food up from the ground. Either pick it up yourself, or move a distance away so he cannot get it.

Uses for Heeling

Again, the most obvious use for the heeling exercise is to be able to walk with Louis in a crowded area, keeping him next to you and under your control at all times. Once Louis understands both "Heel" and "Don't pull," you can mix the two commands. If I am walking with my dog on leash in the don't pull position and someone comes toward me on the sidewalk, I call the dog to heel position until we are past. Then I release him to wander a bit with an "O.K.! Don't pull." Similarly, when my dog is off leash on the quiet country road, if I hear a car, I immediately say "Heel," and keep the dog walking in the heel position until the car passes. This is only to be used when traffic is infrequent. Otherwise, keep Louis on-leash.

QUICK REVIEW

Behavior: Heeling

Cue Words: Louis, Heel. Louis, Sit or Louis, Stop.

1. Dog is held in place with the leash next to trainer's leg, and food is used to keep dog's attention on trainer.
2. Dog is either stopped in a stand or placed in a sit every time trainer stops.
3. Leash is gradually loosened and dog stays in position.
4. Dog stops and/or sits automatically when trainer stops.
5. Proof-training.

13

Confinement

An important part of solving behavioral problems can be teaching your pet to accept confinement for certain periods of time. The best way to accomplish this is with the use of a portable dog kennel or dog crate. I can hear my students when I introduce this topic in training class. They exclaim, "I'm not putting *my* dog in a *box*. That's cruel!" I love to hear the new tune they sing when they have finally been convinced to try the crate. "Why didn't you *tell* me? Crates are *wonderful!*"

The dog is by nature a denning animal. To be confined in a limited space is not mentally stressful once the dog has been given time to adjust. There is always at least one crate standing in my house and I will often find one of my dogs sleeping in the crate with the door open. The crate is the dog's own space where he can be safe and quiet. I use the crate when the dog and I need "out-time" because one of us is driving the other crazy. It is never used for punishment. The best proof I have seen that dogs like to curl up in small spaces took place in the home of a professional breeder I know. This woman breeds one large (sixty-eighty pounds) breed and one small (ten-fifteen pounds) breed and has crates in both sizes. Invariably, the large dogs would try to stuff themselves into the small dogs' crates, which made for some pretty funny scenes. The small dogs rarely curled up in the large crates. The crate can be considered similar to a playpen: a place where a very young creature can be safely confined when not under the direct and immediate supervision of a responsible adult.

There are three types of crates: the wire mesh crate, the fiberglass or airline crate, and the homemade variety. The cost varies with the size and quality of the crate. The wire crates allow more air to circulate and can be cooler in summer, but conversely, can be drafty in winter. Most fold down flat for storage or carrying. The fiberglass crates can be too hot for extremely heavy-coated dogs, but are otherwise a good choice. They are easily washable, light in weight, and can be taken apart to serve as a dog bed. These crates used to come with a good piece of pegboard in the bottom, but that appears to have gone the way of a fifth-wheel spare-tire in your new car. Either cut a piece of pegboard or very heavy cardboard to fit, or pad the bottom heavily, as no dog could be comfortable lying on the dents and bumps of molded plastic on the bottom of these crates. The homemade variety can be made of wire, wood, or a combination of the two. The crate should be large enough for the dog to lie down comfortably and tall enough that he can stand up but not necessarily raise his head. Bigger is not better: fit the crate to the dog.

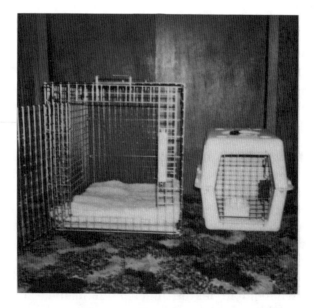

Fig. 13-1. There are two types of crates that can be purchased, a wire mesh crate or a fiberglass crate.

CRATE TRAINING

To teach the dog to accept the crate, set it up in a corner of the kitchen or bedroom. Your children will immediately occupy it. Remove them and put the dog's favorite treat or toy in the crate. Allow the dog to explore the crate. If he goes in to get the treat or toy, praise him. Repeat the procedure until he will go in readily. Now feed him in the crate, with the door open. After a few days, feed him in the crate with the door closed. You may have to stand nearby if he is feeling anxious. Once the dog accepts the crate comfortably, gradually extend the time he spends in it until he can be left for as long as five hours by himself. You can buy a special water dish that attaches to the side of the crate. My dogs consider these a real challenge and work many hours figuring out how to detach them and dump the water on themselves, then they give me accusing looks because they are thirsty. I do not believe in crating dogs regularly for an entire work day without a walk to relieve themselves and stretch. In an emergency, however, a healthy adult dog can tolerate eight or nine hours in a crate—but only when absolutely necessary. I also crate puppies and adults new to my house at night. I place the crate next to my bed so I can hear if the puppy wakes up and is restless or cries to go out. No healthy puppy wants to soil its own bed, so by confining the puppy to the crate I encourage his natural tendency to stay clean. You would be surprised how this speeds up housebreaking. I have found that if I get up once or twice during the night with the crated puppy for the first week or so, by the age of eight to nine weeks, some puppies are able to stay dry all night. (But you'd better hustle them outside or to their papers by the dawn's early light.) For the adult dog the crate not only prevents housesoiling, common in a new environment, but also prevents destructive behavior. How pleasant to wake up or come home to a house that is as I left it, with no chewed up furniture or carpeting. The dog has had a long, restful nap, or played quietly with his toys (which I remembered to leave in the crate with him). I can release the dog with a sincere feeling of welcome on both sides. After a quick trip outside, we are ready to enjoy each other's company with no recriminations for damage done. The first few nights an adult dog is kept in the crate next to my bed, a few words of reassurance and a scratch on the head through the crate mesh will quickly calm any whimpering. Once a dog is accustomed to the crate, any barking or whining is dealt with by either smacking the side of the crate and a firm ''Quiet!'' or by squirting the dog with cold water from a squirt gun or spray bottle, accompanied by the same word. Obviously, before the dog is reprimanded you must be certain he is not fussing because he needs to go out.

A Few Benefits of Crate Training

When I travel with my crate-trained dog, I can take him places he might otherwise be unwelcome. If I visit a non-doggy acquaintance, that person is grateful to know that my dog will be crated at night and under my control during the day. Some motel owners will allow a crated dog, but not an uncrated one.

Should the dog have to be left overnight at the vet's office or confined during recovery from an illness or surgery, the crate-trained dog will accept such confinement as a matter of course and will not experience additional stress because of it. Similarly, should you have occasion to fly your dog somewhere, the familiarity of his own crate will help make the trip a little less frightening.

CAR TRAVEL

The crate serves as a seat belt for a dog riding in a car. If I am going any distance at all, or travelling with a puppy or an untrained adult, the dog is crated. The crate keeps the animal safe and out from under my feet or in some other distracting and potentially dangerous spot. We have seen that one of the uses for the down-stay (chapter 10) is to keep the dog under control when he is riding in the car. Untrained, unrestrained dogs cause accidents when they jump in the driver's lap, get between the driver's feet, or distract the driver who has to take his eyes off the road to discipline a bouncing pet. Drivers who permit untrained dogs to roam at will create a dangerous situation in the car. I cringe when I see a car with a dog's head sticking out the window. Not only can gravel and debris blow into the dog's eyes and ears, but in a collision, the dog is at far more risk of injury when his head is hanging out the window. As to the people who allow their dogs to hang their entire bodies out of the window, balancing precariously and usually barking madly at passing cars, I just try to get in front of such drivers, so I won't be the one to run over the dog when it falls out into traffic. Similarly, I cringe whenever I see a dog riding in the back of an open pickup truck. This seems to be a macho fad, at least in the West. Often these trucks are just open flatbeds, and sometimes assorted children share the platform with the dog—all desperately clinging to whatever they can hold onto. One statistic I read indicated that 200,000 dogs were killed or injured annually riding unattended in open pickup trucks. A dog can jump out of the truck bed unexpectedly, even when he has ridden there without incident for long periods of time. He can be thrown out (especially those dogs who perch on the side of the truck to watch or bark at what is going past) when the truck hits a bump. Then, if he was not injured in falling or jumping out of the truck, the dog is running, panicked in traffic, where he is likely to be hit or cause an accident as drivers try to avoid him. If you can't take the dog in the cab with you, leave him at home. Or at least put him in a crate and tie the crate down. I have seen some giant breeds (Great Danes, Irish Wolfhounds, St. Bernards) ride safely in special harnesses attached to the sides of the truck, but this is an expensive and rather awkward option. If you choose to try it, be sure the dog has some sort of protection from the weather. Your best bet is to put the dog in the truck cab, or leave him at home.

Fig. 13-2. The dog crate keeps the dog safe in the car.

14

Thoughts on Canine Character

Some dogs, as we have previously noted, are simply easier to train than others. While there are exceptions to the generalizations I am about to make, my years of experience have led me to expect certain types of responses from certain breeds of dogs. I want to share some of my observations with you, and also note some health considerations (such as problems with hips and eyes) which may effect trainability. See if you can recognize your dog in these quick portraits. Think about the implications for training of dogs with short attention spans or a propensity to push for alpha position.

THE GUARD BREEDS

These include the dogs that were bred specifically to guard and protect people and/or property, including livestock. They include the Mastiff and Bullmastiff, the Rottweiler, the Doberman Pinscher, the Boxer, the German Shepherd Dog, the Akita, the Giant and Standard Schnauzer, and the rare Komondor, among others. These are the dogs that will be most likely to contend with their owners for pack leadership, probably at an early age. The males will often continue to test for dominance throughout their lives (remember Tora the Akita?). Start training these dogs as early as possible. They may require an occasional pain avoidance correction because of their continued testing of their owners. Most of them will show a natural propensity to guard their people, especially children, and their surroundings. With those they know, they should be friendly and affectionate. It is fine to encourage guarding behavior in one of these dogs, in terms of being watchful and letting you

Fig. 14-1. Doberman Pinschers and German Shepherds are two of the guard breeds who naturally tend to push for dominance. Be prepared to establish yourself as the alpha figure.

know when there is something unusual going on, but be sure you can turn off the behavior by using brief praise and then enforcing an obedience command to re-assert your control. For example, Schultz the Rottweiler goes to the front door and barks or growls. You praise him and (assuming he has been trained) put him on a sit-stay and open the door. When the callers have been admitted or sent away, release him and praise him. He has done his job, but must defer to your judgment as to whether or not he should remain on guard.

The guard breeds are generally super with children, tolerating lots of poking and pinching. They can become protective of "their" kids, however, and show aggression when other children are roughhousing.

Many of these breeds have high incidences of hip dysplasia, partly related to their size (see p. 146). The mastiff-related breeds (those with small dropped-ears, blocky heads and blunt muzzles) are also more prone to some types of cancer than other breeds.

Fig. 14-2. The Boxer and other Mastiff-type breeds are excellent with children, but may also push adults for alpha position. Photo by B.J. Augello.

THE SPITZ BREEDS

These are the dogs with fox-like faces, pointy ears, curly tails and thick coats. They include the Alaskan Malamute, the Siberian Husky, the Norwegian Elkhound, the Keeshond, the Chow, the Pomeranian, the Schipperke, the Eskimo Dog or American Spitz and others. The Akita is also a Spitz breed. These dogs were bred in Northern climates and originally used to pull sleds and to guard property.

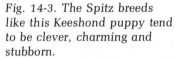

Fig. 14-3. The Spitz breeds like this Keeshond puppy tend to be clever, charming and stubborn.

They tend to be independent, stubborn, and not terribly interested in pleasing their human companions. They often resent corrections and do not learn well through pain avoidance. The larger Spitz breeds will push to become the pack leader. Use the dominance corrections as needed, but train the obedience exercises with positive reward as outlined in the previous chapters. The Keeshond and the Pomeranian tend to be devilishly bright, constantly looking for mischief and smart enough to find it easily.

THE HUNTING BREEDS

These include Spaniels, Retrievers, Pointing breeds and Hounds. Spaniels are usually loving and affectionate, with plenty of charm for anyone who cares to admire them, but they can be extremely stubborn at times. They tend to respond very well to positive reward training. Many spaniels have a tendency toward hereditary eye problems.

Retrievers are the good-natured hail-fellows of the dog world. Many that I have observed are not overly bright, but most would cheerfully die for their owners or anyone else who asked them to. They are very trainable and are generally willing to work at repetitive tasks. They often prove to be outstanding in obedience competition. Retrievers are ideal family dogs and usually are marvelous with children. Most of them have little or no instinct to guard and will happily show the burglars where the silver is in exchange for a pat on the head.

The Golden and Labrador Retrievers have high incidences of hip dysplasia and hereditary eye problems. Retrievers bred from lines used to complete in field trials (as opposed to personal hunting companions) are usually extremely high-energy dogs and can sometimes be less than good house pets because they are so super-charged.

The pointing breeds, including Setters and Pointers are also generally good-natured fellows with little protective instinct. The lines bred for field trial work tend to have very high energy levels and are frequently unreliable off-leash. Those that are more sedate generally have less powerful hunting instincts.

Hounds were bred to hunt using their sense of smell (the Beagle, Basset, Bloodhound, Coonhound) or of sight (the Greyhound, Whippet, Afghan Hound, Irish Wolfhound, Saluki). They were bred to work independently of man, finding and sometimes stopping game so man could come and make the kill or share in the prize. They can be somewhat difficult to housebreak and are not reliable off-leash without substantial

Fig. 14-4. This Golden Retriever puppy shows the sweetness typical of most retrievers. Photo by Bobbie Christenson.

training. They respond well to positive reward training and tend to tolerate very little pain avoidance work. Depending on the breed, some are warm and friendly and others are aloof, only showing affection to a select few. Every Afghan Hound I have examined in training class or while judging an obedience trial has looked absolutely disgusted that I was actually going to put my plebian hands on his or her body. The hounds have only a limited willingness to please their owners. It is not that they do not love their humans, merely that pleasing them is somewhere down around number twenty-three on their list of important things to do in life.

THE HERDING BREEDS

These dogs were bred to work closely with their owners to control livestock. They include the Collie, the Shetland Sheepdog, the Border Collie, the Corgi, the Australian Shepherd and the Australian Cattle Dog, among others. There are other breeds which carry the title of Shepherd, (the German Shepherd the Old English Sheepdog, e.g.) but whose primary task was guarding the stock rather than herding it. The herding dogs are

Fig. 14-5. The herding breeds like this Border Collie tend to have lots of energy and will get into trouble if they are not given something to do.

generally selective about their human companions, being one-man or one-family dogs. They are excellent with children, and take their herding responsibilities for their two- or four-legged charges very seriously. They are usually bright and willing and rather intense about whatever they do. These dogs seem to have greater attention spans than many other dogs.

Unfortunately, there is a disproportionate number of poor temperaments in the herding breeds. Many are shy and a few aggressive. These breeds must be exposed to lots of different people and places as soon as they have had their puppy shots. Some are prone to hereditary eye problems and/or epilepsy. They tend to be barkers as well.

THE TERRIERS

Terriers—which include the Miniature Schnauzer and the Dachshund—were bred to hunt and kill burrowing animals including rats, mice, foxes, and badgers. Consequently, digging is in their blood and you will be hard-pressed to cure them of this behavior. They are courageous, often to the point of fool-hardiness. They have lots of energy and are perpetually curious.

Fig. 14-6. Terriers tend to be curious and feisty. Photo by Pat Lenahan.

Terriers tend to have a limited ability to concentrate on any one thing because they are so very busy checking out everything else that is going on. They can be stubborn and many of the terrier breeds go around with chips on their shoulders, easily provoked to fight with other dogs. People often have difficulty maintaining more than two terriers together without either constant vigilance or constant bloodshed. Terriers respond well to a mixture of positive reward and pain avoidance training. Because of their feistiness they often need reminders of who is alpha in the house. They are reasonably willing to please their owners, but are highly distractable. Terriers tend to be noisy. to be noisy.

THE TOY BREEDS

Many toy dogs show perpetual juvenile physical and emotional characteristics: they never really grow up. This is part of their appeal, in that they become permanent babies for their owners. Most of the behavioral problems experienced by toy dogs are a direct result of being spoiled by their owners, who do not allow them to be dogs. Depending on the breed, they tend to have a high incidence of epilepsy and knee problems (slipping stifles). Toy dogs' teeth require special attention or they are likely to lose them at an early age.

POODLES

Poodles in all sizes tend to be clowns. They should be bright and curious. They have a strong stubborn streak which can be quickly brought to the fore by pain avoidance training. Positive reward training makes them much more cooperative. The poodles I have observed seem to be very willing to please their owners. They are easily bored and will test their humans to see how much they can get away with. A friend of mine speaks knowingly of "the black heart of the apricot poodle."

PERSONALITY TYPES

While these generalizations regarding the different breeds of dogs may prepare you to expect certain responses as outlined, you must observe and consider your dog's individual character and personality as you proceed with training. Is your dog bright and perky, or aloof, or shy and fearful? Do you suspect your dog is less than a genius? There is as much variation in canine intelligence as there is in human intelligence. To maximize the time you are investing in training your dog, use the following information to form a picture of how your dog's individual personality will affect his ability to learn. I have included some advice on things you may want to emphasize or minimize as you work with your particular dog.

The Shy Dog

A dog becomes shy either by inheriting a poor temperament or by the breeder or owner's failure to expose the dog to as many environments and people as possible when he was young and impressionable (from seven to sixteen weeks of age). The latter problem is known as "kennel syndrome" and is very hard to overcome. Most shy dogs are primarily afraid either of people or of places and objects. This is an unreasoning fear and is usually not traceable to a specific incident, as in: "He was abused by a man and now he is afraid of all men." Probably the propensity for shyness was there and was certainly not helped by any mistreatment. I have seen dogs with backgrounds of serious abuse and neglect that bounce back from the negative experiences and become well-adjusted pets once they are placed in loving homes. I have seen, and owned, others that were never normal in spite of extensive and careful socialization and care.

To train the shy dog first of all remember that he *is* shy. You may have quite a bit of success in overcoming his spooky reactions, but he will never be as reliable as some other dogs because his unreasoning fear can crop up at any time and cause him to panic. Be especially cautious about working the shy dog off-leash. Never reward the spooky behavior by reassuring and petting. You are not comforting your shy dog—you are telling him that spooky behavior will be rewarded with petting and kind words. Be matter-of-fact in your training. When Louis shies from a person or an object, gently guide him up to whatever scared him and hold him firmly in a sit until he relaxes. You may pat or talk to the person or object (if you don't mind some strange looks) to show Louis that you are not afraid of it. Do not praise or reward Louis until he relaxes enough to do a brief on-leash sit-stay near the object of his fear. Then reward and praise enthusiastically. If Louis is afraid of people, try having everyone he meets offer him a treat. If he is not interested, use the sit-stay as outlined above. Work hard on dog attention. If Louis is watching you he will be less likely to notice scarey things around him. You may need to use a ten to fifteen minute down-stay to introduce Louis to each new level of distraction when you start proof-training him. Start each training session in a new place with this exercise. Be sure any corrections during the down-stay are slow and deliberate, rather than hurried and abrupt. Don't use Louis's shyness as an excuse not to train him to whatever level of proficiency you want to reach. The training itself, outlining clearly for Louis what is expected of him and setting consistent limits to his behavior, can increase his confidence as well as give you control of him. Finally, do neuter your spook. It will calm him down to some degree and will prevent him from producing more spooks.

The Wimp

This is the opposite of the alpha dog, and in fact, may have been at the bottom of the pack when the order of dominance was established in his litter. This dog melts whenever he receives any type of correction, showing all kinds of submissive behavior, up to and including submissive urination. Proceed slowly with the wimp, extending the period in which you prevent him from making mistakes, so that you can avoid correction as much as possible. When you do administer a pop on the collar with the leash, give the cue word in a cheerful voice rather than a gruff tone. Some wimps develop more confidence with training and with age, but they can never tolerate rough training.

The Hyper Dog

This is the high-energy dog that is always busy. If you don't occupy him with training, he will find destructive ways to occupy himself. Some breeds are bred to be hypes. If you don't like dogs that are constantly on the go, don't buy a terrier or a herding dog. They are bred to work energetically, so having this type of nature is correct for them whether you can stand to live with it or not. Keep your training session short when you start working with your hyper dog. Allow him time to build his attention span. Maintain a calm demeanor at all times as you don't need to rev this dog up with your own energy. Keep your voice quiet and your body motions slow and deliberate. Work hard on dog attention. Do not use the pinch collar or the choke chain on the hype. These collars tend to stimulate a dog. Either use the plain, buckle collar or try to buy or make a parachute cord collar. Parachute cord can be found at army surplus stores. It is a very narrow, slick nylon cord (see fig. 147) which has a calming effect when fitted high on the dog's neck and used as a choke collar. I am not sure why this is true but it works in many cases to bring the hype down to earth. You do not have to use a heavy hand with this collar even though it is a pain avoidance device. Some of the better pet stores carry these collars. Do not confuse them with the regular thick nylon choke collars which do not produce the calming effect.

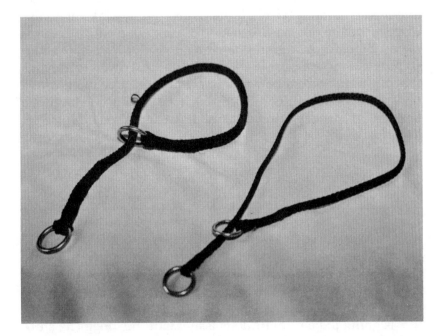

Fig. 14-7. *The regular nylon choke collar (on the left) is twice as thick as the parachute cord collar.*

The Dumb Dog

This is one of the more frustrating dogs to train because it takes so long for the dog to make the connection between the cue word and the desired behavior. They key word here is patience and more patience. Be very slow to correct the dumb dog, as he really will not understand why you are correcting him. Show him what you want until you can't bear to do it again. Then show him what you want for at least an additional week before administering a correction. Don't introduce more than one new thing in any lesson. Check each thing off in this book as the dog learns it, and be careful not to demand too much too soon.

The Stubborn Dog

This is the dog that wants to call the shots and that only gets worse with pain-avoidance corrections. Corrections make him more resistant. Withholding praise and reward sometimes works once the dog has learned to expect the positive induce-ments. Sometimes, the stubborn dog doesn't give a hoot about your praise and simply says, "No!, I won't." Try not to provoke this dog's stubbornness every time you train. Use the positive reward methods outlined in this book. Once this dog has done an exercise correctly, do not repeat it. Go on to something else. You may come back to the first exercise later in the training session. If you must correct beyond the pop on the buckle collar, use a quick scruff-shake rather than a pain-avoidance correc-tion. Isolate this dog for an hour before each training session if you can. Keep proof-training to a minimum, and work slowly so as to avoid the need for much correction. Some dogs are will-ing to do certain exercises but balk at others. Work the problem exercise separately so you and the dog can honestly feel good about most of your training sessions. If you have read this book carefully, you are probably thinking that some of the stubborn-ness is related to dominance. You are absolutely correct, and this is going to be a continuous issue with this dog. The stub-born dog is not usually one that growls or snaps to show his dominance; he merely resists. Be patient and observe him carefully so you will know when he honestly doesn't understand and when he is telling you to get lost. The spitz breeds are often in this category.

The Alpha (Aggressive) Dog

Be sure you have done what you can to settle the dominance issue with this dog before you start training. Be prepared for some ongoing confrontations, but expect to put less effort into your dominance corrections as training progresses. That is, you may have to hold Louis in the take down position for three or four long minutes the first time he challenges you, until he stops growling. By the sixth or seventh confrontation, a quick scruff-shake may be enough to settle him down. Do not overlook *any* challenge to your leadership. Be watchful for aggressive behavior in situations that increase tension, such as teaching the down, or adding distraction when proof-training. Some aggressive dogs will only show that side of their characters when under stress. Use as much of the positive reward method as you can, but be careful when introducing anything new.

Do neuter this dog. It may make a drastic improvement in his or her temperament. Females can be as aggressive as males. The most alpha dog I have ever met was a female Border Collie I dog sat for one enlightening week. This animal was a top-scoring obedience trial winner and a well-mannered house pet—in her own home. When she arrived at my house, she walked in and promptly had my larger dogs grovelling in the dirt. She lifted her leg and wet on my sofa and then before I could grab her, jumped onto the kitchen table to help herself to a snack. When I yanked her off the table, she growled at me. We had a serious discussion about who was in charge, which we had to repeat every morning for the length of her visit. So much for the sweet, tractable temperament of the female.

There are some other house rules that will help you get along with the aggressive dog. Use thirty-minute down-stays every day to maintain your alpha position. Do not pet the dog for more than five seconds, no matter how he nudges your hand. Make him do something (sit, down, come) to earn his petting. Give him only one toy to play with at a time. Everything else is yours. Do not step over or around him when you want to get by. Make him get out of your way. Do not roughhouse with this dog. Play only retrieving games with him and be sure he returns the ball or Frisbee to you. Put him on-leash if necessary. The Border Collie described above would catch the Frisbee if she could and then run off with it and chew it, giving me challenging looks over her shoulder. If she couldn't catch it, she would intimidate the dog that had caught it, take it from him, and run off with it.

The Smart Dog

There are two types of smart dogs: the willing and the wily, or rottenhearted smart dog. If you have the first type, lucky you. This is the dog described in most training books. You show the dog how to do something and he will cheerfully repeat it forever. These dogs are few and far between, but they are nice to have. Frequently they need almost no formal training, apparently picking up what you want them to do by telepathy or osmosis.

The wily smart dog is a definite challenge. He can be exasperating, but he is always fun. He is not challenging you for dominance, he is just showing you variations on training you failed to think of. Don't repeat an exercise with this dog once he has done it correctly. That is merely an invitation to him to do it differently. Try not to correct this dog for making a mistake. Instead, withhold praise and rewards and help him do it right. This is a dog that needs lots of proof-training, not because he doesn't understand what you want, but because he doesn't believe you are going to require his obedience all the time. He will test you to see if he has to perform under any new circumstances. Keep new things coming, as this dog will become bored easily. Teach him tricks as well as his obedience lessons. Use food rewards to keep him interested when you work on something he knows. Once he shows you he understands an exercise, do not work on it every day. Every third or fourth day is plenty. Variety is the key for this dog, plus a sense of humor on the part of the owner.

The Impossible Dog

I must state flatly that there are dogs that cannot be lived with no matter how much training and love you put into them.

The dog whose behavior is totally unpredictable is one. This dog may be loving and affectionate one minute, shy the next, and aggressive the next, with no apparent reason and no warning of the change.

Another is the dog that is so shy that no amount of training makes a difference. This dog is never at ease, even in his own home with only you present. There is no joy in this dog's life, and he is a never ending drain on your energy and patience, with no reward in the form of improved behavior to compensate. He is not able to be your companion.

Yet another is the aggressive dog that continues to be dangerous to you and/or to everyone around him. This dog does not respond to training, no matter how faithfully and how long it is done. Even a professional trainer can only make a temporary dent in this dog's armor.

I am aware that you love your dog, or you would not have bothered to read this book and attempted to train the dog. In spite of your affection for the animal, you must realize that these types of dogs bring no pleasure to themselves or to anyone around them. Life for them is a miserable experience. You cannot give these dogs away because they would have the same problems in any environment. The only reasonable course of action for any of these dogs is to take the dog to your veterinarian and have it humanely enthanized (put to sleep). Grieve for the animal and then, when you are ready, start again. Make a better choice of temperament this time and raise the dog to be a sane, safe, and happy companion.

15

Responsible
Dog Ownership

T here are many aspects to being a responsible pet owner. Obedience training is only one aspect. Some others you will want to think about include health, grooming, exercise, and control of reproduction.

YOUR DOG'S HEALTH

When you do not feel well physically it affects your mental state. If you have sore muscles or an upset stomach it is much harder for you to concentrate, especially if you are trying to learn something new. This holds equally true for your dog. Not only is it harder for him to learn when he is not in optimum health, but some problems which appear to relate to behavior can actually be undiagnosed health problems. For example, when my Border Collie, Dave, was a young puppy he appeared to be having a great deal of difficulty with housebreaking. I knew this was unusual for this breed as they are very bright and willing dogs and generally learn the rules much more quickly than the average dog. A trip to the vet proved that there was a minor medical problem. After a few days' medication, housebreaking was accomplished and we were able to move on to other things. Most professional trainers and dog behaviorists routinely insist that a dog be checked by a veterinarian before investigating any behavior problems.

A healthy dog has clear bright eyes and a shine to his coat. He moves comfortably with a reasonably even gait. He is interested in what is going on around him and has a consistently good appetite for regular dog food (unless he has been taught to eat people food). How can you tell if your dog is sick? There are obvious signs of distress, such as a limp, vomiting, diarrhea, coughing or choking, swelling, rubbing or pawing at the eyes or ears, bleeding, loss of appetite or excessive water consumption. A dog that is ill will be likely to tire easily, and have little energy for play. This is not to be confused with the natural slowing down of the older dog, although many senior canines maintain high energy levels throughout their lives. Sometimes, there are no obvious signs to warn you that your pet is sick. His appetite may disappear, although there are some dogs that would not miss a meal as long as they could physically drag themselves to the food. Another non-acute sign of illness is continued discharge from the dog's eyes or nose. It is not true, by the way, that a dog is healthy if his nose is cold and wet.

Fig. 15-1. A healthy dog is bright, active and curious.

You can only see these signs of illness in your dog if you observe him regularly and make a mental note of how he looks and acts when he is healthy. Regular veterinary care is also a must. I know there are many dogs that survive to advanced ages without ever seeing a veterinarian, but you must understand that those dogs are not only exceptionally hearty, they are exceptionally *lucky.* Rabies and distemper are still around, along with a number of less familiar, but no less deadly illnesses, which can be prevented with proper inoculations. An annual visit to the vet should include "the shots" and a general checkup. Your vet will establish a record of your dog's health so that he or she will have a baseline from which to judge any problems or changes you may report. Some people labor under the mistaken notion that the shots given to a new puppy are sufficient to protect it for life. This is *not true.* See the chart below for the types of shots needed and when they should be given.

TYPE OF INNOCULATION	BOOSTER (ADDITIONAL SHOTS) NEEDED	HOW OFTEN
1. Rabies	Yes	Generally every 3 years. Some communities require annual shots for licensing.
2. Distemper	Yes	Annually
3. Infectious Canine Hepatitis	Yes	Annually
4. Leptospirosis	Yes	Annually
5. Parvovirus	Yes	Annually
6. Parainfluenza (Kennel Cough)	Yes	Annually
7. Bordatella (a new intranasal kennel cough vaccine)	Yes	Annually

NOTE: Numbers 2 through 6 are usually given together in one injection.

As part of your picture of how your dog looks when he is healthy, make a note of his normal temperature and pulse and keep it with his record of inoculations. The normal temperature for a dog is 101—102.5 ° F. Take the temperature when the dog has been resting for a while, not when he has been exercising vigorously. The temperature is taken rectally, and most dogs will not raise more than a minor objection to the process. Buy Fido his own thermometer and shake it down. Dip the business end in some Vaseline®. Grip the base of the dog's tail and gently pull the tail straight up (pointing to the ceiling). The dog can be standing or lying down (in which case the tail is held parallel with the floor) and you may want someone to help hold him until you both survive the first attempt. Insert the thermometer half-way into the rectum, and hold it there for two minutes. Remove it, wipe if off and read it.

Your dog's pulse can be found by feeling the artery inside his thigh. Count the beats for ten seconds and multiply by six. The normal resting pulse rate for a dog varies from 60 to 130 per minute depending on the size of the dog. The average size dog has a pulse rate of 80 to 100 per minute. Smaller dogs tend to have higher pulse rates.

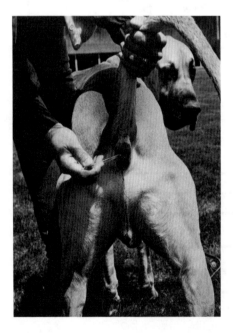

Fig. 15-2. Taking the temperature. The dog tolerates this, although not necessarily cheerfully.

If you think your dog is ill, take his temperature and pulse before calling the vet. This will help the vet assess the seriousness of the dog's condition so he or she can tell you if an immediate visit is needed or not.

If your vet prescribes medication, be sure to follow the instructions for administration. Don't be surprised that the costs for medications are as high as those your doctor prescribes for you. They may be the same medications, especially in the case of antibiotics. If you must give a dog a pill, you may try hiding the pill in some cheese, raw ground beef or peanut butter. Watch the dog carefully for a few minutes, as some dogs are experts at pill extracting and will fool you and spit the pill out while enjoying the treat. The surest way to give a pill is to open the dog's mouth and insert the pill as far back in the dog's throat as possible. Close the mouth and hold the chin up so the dog cannot spit the pill back at you. Stroke the dog's throat or blow gently into his nose until he swallows. You can tell he has swallowed by watching for his tongue to protrude. Liquid medicine is easiest to give with a large syringe (no needle) designed for this purpose. The method is the same. Squirt the liquid as far back in the dog's throat as possible. Or, pull the side of the lower lip out to form a pouch, tilt the dog's head up and trickle the liquid into the pouch.

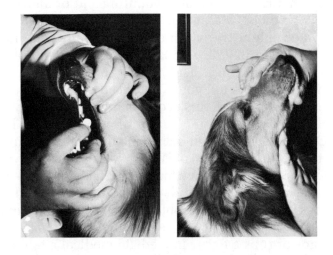

Fig. 15-3. Giving medication in pill form.

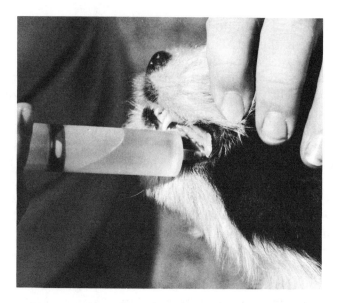

Fig. 15-4. Giving liquid medication with a syringe.

COMMON PROBLEMS

Stomach Problems

If you notice an incident of vomiting and/or diarrhea, and if there is no blood present and if the dog otherwise appears healthy, you might try withholding any additional food for twenty-four hours (but do give small regular amounts of water). This is not harmful to a healthy dog in spite of what those pleading brown eyes tell you. Then, feed the dog a bland diet for the next forty-eight hours. You can buy prescription canned or kibbled food called "I/D" from your veterinarian to keep on hand. Or you can make your own bland diet by combining plain boiled rice or farina (Cream of Wheat®), low fat cottage cheese, and boiled ground beef from which all the fat has been skimmed. Then, over the next several days, gradually re-introduce the dog's regular food. If the problems recur, take the dog, with a small stool specimen, to the vet. If at any time the dog shows other signs or runs a fever, immediate medical attention is in order.

Bloat and Torsion

Stomach dilation, commonly known as "bloat" is most common in large, deep chested dogs. It can happen to any dog. In bloat, gas is trapped in the stomach and the stomach distends visibly. The dog will show increasing discomfort in the form of restlessness, an inability to remain in one position for long, panting, unproductive vomiting and sometimes crying or whining. This is an *EXTREME EMERGENCY* and you must rush your dog to the nearest vet immediately. Without treatment the dog is likely to die a painful death. At times, bloat is followed by a gastric torsion, in which the stomach actually twists. If the dog is not treated within a few hours, it will die. The cause of this condition is not known, but some theories link it to certain types of food, and some experts believe there is a hereditary component. Some veterinarians suggest water be restricted immediately after the dog has eaten and that the dog not be allowed to exercise vigorously for at least one hour after eating as preventive measures.

Parasites

Internal—There are many types of parasites, often generically and inaccurately called "worms," that can affect your pet. Some can be seen in the stools, either looking like pieces of rice (tapeworm) or like rubber bands (roundworms). Most, such as hookworms, whipworms, and Giardia are only detectable by placing a stool specimen under the microscope. Common signs of parasite infestation include intermittent soft stools (not necessarily diarrhea), poor coat condition, bloated abdomen, and weight loss in spite of increased food intake. If you think your dog has parasites, take a stool specimen to the vet. DO NOT attempt to worm the dog yourself with over-the-counter preparations or home remedies. The vet will give you the proper medication in the proper dosage for your dog. Self-medication can be extremely dangerous.

Most types of parasites can make your dog uncomfortable and weaken it to some degree. However, one type is exceptionally dangerous and can cripple or kill your pet: heartworm. This parasite can only be detected accurately through bloodwork and the dog must be treated immediately with ongoing medical supervision. Heartworm is spread by mosquitoes and most dogs should be taking a medication (either a pill or a powder to put on the food) to prevent infestation during the mosquito season. The medication can *only* be given safely to dogs that are free of the parasite, however, so you *must* have the dog checked before starting preventive treatment.

External—The most common external parasites affecting dogs are fleas, ticks, lice, and mange mites. Some of these can be seen by the owner (and some will be happy to live on the owner as well as the dog) and some are not visible without magnification. If your dog scratches constantly, has excessive or patchy hair loss, or has obvious sores on his skin, take him to the vet for diagnosis. Most vets would appreciate your leaving your dog in the car until it is his turn, especially if he has visible parasites. Treatment usually consists of a series of baths for the dog and some type of fumigation for the house. In some areas of the country this is an on-going battle and very frustrating for all parties (except the parasites) involved.

Ear mites are another common external parasite. A dog with ear mites will paw at his ears, or rub his head on the ground frequently, or will shake his head constantly. These signs can also indicate a foreign body in the ear, such as a seed or pebble. Either condition requires veterinary attention and not home remedies. There will be a dark, smelly, waxy substance in the ears when there are mites and the ears may be very sensitive to your touch, so handle them carefully.

Seizures

Dogs have seizures similar to those seen in people. Seizures can be a sign of epilepsy, or of some other illness, or poisoning. Any dog that has convulsions (grand-mal type seizures) requires immediate veterinary attention. Epileptic seizures can frequently be controlled with medication.

Eyes

Be especially careful if your dog has either protruding eyes (the Boston Terrier, Pug, Pekingese, or mixes of those breeds) or drooping eyelids (Bassets and other hounds), as these dogs will be most prone to eye problems. Signs of eye problems include reddening of the eyes, swelling, discharge, and the dog's rubbing or pawing his eyes. You may gently flush the eyes with warm water, but do not wait long to seek medical attention. A surprising number of dogs lose part or all of their vision due to a number of hereditary diseases as well as to diseases of old age. Blind dogs can cope quite successfully if their environment is not changed very often.

Lameness

If your dog develops a limp, gently examine his feet and legs for cuts, sores or foreign objects. If there is no obvious cause, restrict the dog's exercise for a day or two (this is not difficult with a trained dog). If the lameness does not go away, it is time for a trip to the vet. If the dog completely avoids putting his sore leg down, there may be a fracture present, in which case immediate veterinary attention is in order.

Hip Dysplasia

This malformation of the hip joints is found in many breeds and mixes of various breeds. In medium to large breeds, it can be a crippling problem, causing constant pain for the dog. It is generally thought that this condition is hereditary in nature. It is not an illness that a dog can "catch" anymore than you can "catch" someone else's bad knee. The most common signs of hip dysplasia are that the dog has difficulty getting up (especially when the weather is cold and damp), the rear end of the dog appears much thinner than the front (as though it were wasting away), and the dog moves its rear feet together in a "bunny hop," rather than alternating feet when walking or trotting. There is treatment for this condition, ranging from pain control to rather expensive orthopedic surgery. Because of the degree of pain involved, some dogs may need to be euthanized at a relatively early age. There are many severely dysplastic dogs that show no clinical signs of disease. The only way to be certain is through an x-ray of the dog's hips. If you suspect something is wrong, check with your veterinarian.

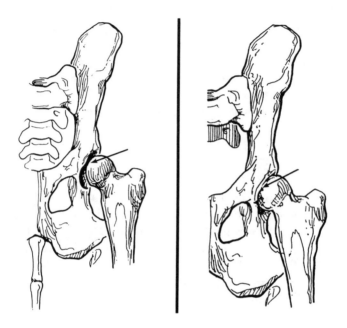

Fig. 15-5. A Dysplastic hip joint (left) and a normal hip (right). Note how the joint fits poorly in the socket of the dysplastic hip.

Respiratory Illness

Dogs are fortunate in that they do not experience annoying head colds. They can, however, get pneumonia, tonsilitis, and a series of nasty bugs commonly labeled "kennel cough." If your dog actually coughs (usually a hacking cough that sounds like he is starting to vomit), wheezes, or is having any obvious trouble breathing, a visit to the vet is in order. Generally these signs are accompanied by others such as fever, discharge from the eyes and nose, or loss of appetite. Incidentally, kennel cough is extremely contagious—which is how it got its name, as dogs would contract it after spending time in the kennel—so keep your sick dog isolated until he is well. If you have more than one dog, they will probably pass it around like children and measles.

Weight

I know some fat, happy dogs and some fat, happy people, but I don't think the dogs are getting a fair shake in this case. Most dogs, like most people, feel and look better when they are not significantly overweight. Dogs with respiratory and orthopedic problems suffer far more complications if they are fat. Your dog does not have to contend with the everyday hazards facing people who struggle to control their weight: no fast food joints on the road, no commercials (no, the dog doesn't know when there is a dog food commercial on the TV), no ethnic restaurants. You can control your dog's weight rather easily by limiting his food intake and restricting him to dog food. Dogs can do without much variety in their diets. An occasional treat is acceptable, mainly to make the owner feel better. You can tell if your dog is overweight by feeling his ribs and his hips (the end of the back, above the tail). If you can feel the outline of the bones, with a thin padding of flesh over them, the dog is in good weight. If the only way you could find the ribs is with surgery, your dog is fat. And no, it is not just coat, any more than your own spare tire is "just coat." You do owe your dog his optimal health, and controlling his weight is your responsibility.

Fig. 15-6. It is not fair or safe to allow your dog to remain overweight.

16

Grooming

Part of maintaining your dog's health is keeping him groomed and clean. Regular grooming is part of your ongoing observation of your dog, and allows you to examine him regularly for parasites, wounds, and any unusual conditions. A trained dog is easy to groom and the dog will enjoy the attention and the physical contact.

A clean, unmatted dog is nicer to have around than one that is dirty and smelly. There are several areas which require attention.

COAT

If you have a dog with a long coat, it should be brushed *to the skin* weekly. This requires that you use a good slicker or pin brush and go over the dog an inch at a time, laying the coat flat as you brush each layer. Then take a steel comb and go through the tangly places behind the ears, on the belly, and along the backs of the legs. If you find a mat, try to work it out with your fingers and the end of the comb. If you can't, take a small pair of scissors and carefully cut into the mat several times *without pulling the mat away from the skin.* Groomers tell me this is the most common way people make holes in their dogs. Also, be sure you can see the tips of the scissor blades before you cut. Short-coated dogs can be brushed with a stiff bristle brush.

Your dog should be bathed when he is dirty, using a dog shampoo. Be sure to rinse out all of the soap. Towel dry the dog and brush him thoroughly. Many dogs learn to tolerate a blow dryer. Be sure the dog is completely dry before putting him outside. While many long-haired breeds require periodic trimming and clipping to look their best, it is *never* a good idea to shave the dog to the skin. The coat provides natural insulation from both heat and cold. You can learn to clip or trim your own dog by reading books or by paying a groomer to teach you. Be prepared for your first few attempts to look as though the dog lost a battle with the lawn mower, and take heart: you will improve.

Fig. 16-1. An Assortment of common grooming tools.

Fig. 16-2. Try to work mats out gently with your fingers before using scissors.

Fig. 16-3. *Always brush a long coat in layers, getting all the way to the skin.*

EARS

Clean the dog's ears weekly by reaching in only as far as you can with your fingers, with cotton and a drop of baby oil. Caution: a *drop*—too much oil will leave your dog looking like a punk rocker and will attract dirt. If you have a dog with large, hanging ears, air will not circulate well in them and the dog may be more prone to painful ear infections. Many owners of Basset Hounds and other dogs with heavy ear flaps put a small amount of antibiotic ointment in the ears regularly, and massage it down into the ear by rubbing along the outside of the ear canal. Similarly, dogs with an abundance of hair growing down into the ear canal may have less air flow. You can gently pluck some of this hair out on a regular basis.

TEETH

Your dog's teeth need regular attention. Relatively few dogs will keep their teeth completely clean by chewing on toys or bones or rawhide strips. Most need some help, especially as they age. Small dogs are prone to chronic dental problems, often resulting in loss of teeth at an early age. Dirty teeth cause doggy breath, although that can also be caused by other problems. Look at your dog's teeth, especially the canines (eye teeth) and the rear molars (see p. 75 on how to open the dog's mouth). If there are large deposits of yellow or brown matter on the teeth (dental plaque, similar to what builds up on human teeth), the dog needs to be seen by the vet. If the teeth are very dirty, the vet will anesthetize the dog lightly so the cleaning can be thorough. Even the best trained dog is not likely to ''open wide'' for this procedure. Once the teeth have been cleaned, you can keep them that way by brushing twice a week (yes, you can brush your dog's teeth!) with a soft toothbrush dipped in hydrogen peroxide or salt.

Dogs do need hard things to chew, but many vets recommend against giving dogs bones. Aside from the unsanitary nature of an uncooked bone left to ripen in the yard a few days, some dogs can chew off tiny pieces of bone which gather in the intestine and cause terrible constipation. A better solution for long-term chewing is a *Nylabone®*, available from the pet store in several shapes and sizes, and even in several flavors.

Fig. 16-4. *The veterinarian will scale the tartar deposits off the dog's teeth.*

These toys are practically indestructible and can be washed safely. Rawhide chews are also good, but some dogs seem to devour them so quickly that the benefit to their teeth is doubtful. If your dog breaks or chips a tooth, take him to the vet, as the tooth may need to be ground smooth or removed.

FEET

Look at your dog's feet. Are his toenails so long that they curve under, or so long that they force his toes to spread apart when he stands on a hard surface? If so, you must cut them back. Some people believe that active dogs wear their nails back naturally. Not necessarily. I have know guide dogs for the blind that walked long distances on concrete sidewalks, but whose nails still needed to be trimmed regularly. Long nails are more apt to break and be torn off. The dog's feet can be permanently spread if the nails are left too long. We even hear horror stories about dogs whose nails grow so long they curve around under the feet and grow into the pads of the feet.

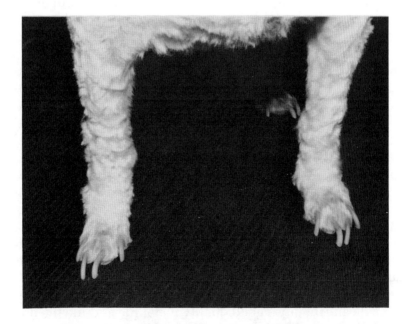

Fig. 16-5. A horrible example of untrimmed toenails. See how the feet are spread. Photo by Marcy Haire.

Fig. 16-6. *Well-cared for feet - toenails cut short, hair on the feet trimmed.*

Nail care is simple. Buy a good set of dog nail clippers (the cheap ones, often seen in supermarkets, cause the nails to split). For a toy dog, you can use a human-type nail clipper. Look at the nail and notice where the pink vein is visible. Do not cut into that vein, if possible, as it will bleed and will cause the dog some discomfort. Insert the white tip of the nail into the hole in the clippers and squeeze (see fig. 16-6). You are less likely to have a problem if you remove a little at a time. If the dog's nails are very long, you will have to do this every three days until the pink vein (the "quick") recedes so you can cut the nails without bleeding. The dog's nails are short enough if the ends do not touch the ground when the dog is standing on a hard surface. "But," you protest, "my dog has *black* nails!" In that case, you will work by touch. The dead part of the nail feels dry and rough. As you start to approach the quick, the texture of the nail will become moist and slightly rubbery. Stop cutting there. This technique is simple and I have taught it to visually impaired people with total success. If you are still feeling squeamish, buy a good quality metal file and file the dog's nails short. It will take quite a bit longer, but cannot hurt the dog. It is a good idea to touch up the end of the nails with a file after clipping to remove any rough edges that can catch in carpeting. If you should nick the vein, you can use a styptic pencil or an ice cube to stop the bleeding. Do not panic, as this will cause the dog to panic. Dogs do not bleed to death from being "quicked."

After the nails are trimmed, take a small pair of scissors and carefully cut away all of the hair between the pads of the feet. This prevents ice and mud-balls from forming and keeps your floors much cleaner. If you want to complete the job, trim the hair around the foot, holding the scissors against the nails to achieve a smooth line. This may look a bit choppy the first few times you try it, but keep at it. This entire procedure should be done every two weeks, and becomes very automatic. The dog can sit, stand, or lie down, whichever is most comfortable for both of you.

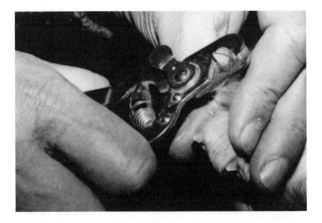

Fig. 16-7. *Cutting the toenails. Trim a little off at a time, being careful not to cut into the vein.*

ANAL GLANDS

When you see your dog scooting along the floor or ground on the base of his tail, he is attempting to expel his anal glands. These are two small sacs set on either side of the anus which normally collect a dark, smelly liquid which may be involved in scent marking for territory identification. When the sacs are full, the dog will scoot to expel them. Frankly, I would prefer not to have this matter embedded in my carpeting. Therefore, three or four times per year, or as soon as I observe the scooting, I expel the glands myself, It is an unaesthetic procedure, but not difficult. If what I am about to describe makes you squeamish, or if you try it and can't succeed, your vet or groomer can do it for you.

Take the dog outside. Grasp the dog's tail at the base and pull up, causing the anus to protrude slightly. With your other hand, padded with a wad of tissue, grasp the sides of the anus and pinch away from the dog's body. You should get a thin dark liquid. If the discharge is thick, bloody or greenish in color, infection may be present, and a trip to the vet is in order. This procedure should not be painful for the dog, although you can hardly expect him to look forward to it.

Fig. 16-8. Expelling the anal glands.

TATTOOING

Dogs should be tattooed for positive identification. This is especially important if you have a dog that is indistinguishable from 5000 similar dogs: i.e., a long-haired, curly-tailed Poodle mix, or a Black Lab, or a Shepherd-Collie mix. Many vets or professional groomers can tattoo any identifying number you wish on the inside of your dog's thigh. Tattoos are sometimes placed in the dog's ear, but the thigh is roomier and is unlikely to be amputated by a dog-napper. The process is essentially painless, in spite of the dramatic performance put on by some dogs. The number can be registered with one of several national registries, and you can put signs on your house or yard stating that the dog is tattooed. Dog thieves will often pass such dogs by, as many laboratories that buy stolen dogs won't accept tattooed specimens. A tattoo is the only permanent definitive identification a dog can wear. It is an inexpensive way to gain a little more security in case your pet is lost.

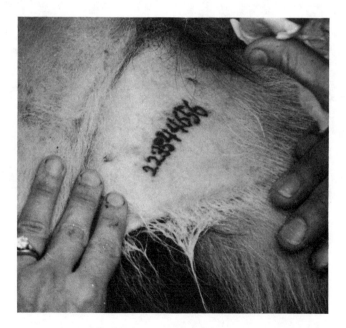

Fig. 16-9. The tattoo is placed on the inside of the thigh and provides permanent identification for your dog.

Fig. 17-1. Raising puppies requires a lot of work, even for small breeds like these Boston Terriers. Photo by Mrs. Pat Jackna.

17

Why Are You Planning To Breed?

Responsible dog ownership involves many facets of your pet's life. The reproductive facet is an important one. Frankly, most breedings that occur should not happen. The American Humane Association estimates that *twenty million* animals were handled by animal shelters and animal control officers in 1983. Of those brought into the shelters, seventy-two percent were euthanized. As many as *fourteen million dogs and cats* were legally killed in this country in 1983. This does not include those hit by cars or dumped somewhere and allowed to starve to death. Apart from the suffering and waste of life, the financial cost of these statistics is overwhelming. And yet people continue to allow their animals to breed.

Let's look at the reasons people allow their dogs to breed:

"We love Poopsie and we want another dog just like her/him."
The odds are against it—even if Poopsie is a purebred. The factors that shape temperament are so involved and complex that it is rare that an individual personality reproduces itself, except that shy and/or nasty dogs do tend to produce more shy and/or nasty dogs. As to physical resemblance, ask a professional breeder how hard it is to reproduce physical type—and be prepared for long, sad tales of unsuccessful attempts to breed another "Champion Whosis." Furthermore, it is not fair to expect a puppy to grow into a replica of its parent. That is as unrealistic as expecting your child to grow up to be exactly like you or to expect two siblings to be exactly alike.

"We want to breed Poopsie because he/she is a purebred."

Purebred only means that you know who the parents were and what they looked like. It has nothing whatsoever to do with quality, health, soundness, etc. It is *not* a reason to breed. People acquire purebred dogs because there is a certain predictability as to size, coat, color and temperament which is not present in the mongrel (or mutt, mixed breed, random-breed, generic or All-American) dog. There is tremendous variation even within each breed. Unless you specifically purchased a breeding-quality purebred (see box), don't breed.

"We spent good money for Poopsie and we want to recover our investment."

Aside from a conflict I feel about thinking of companion animals as nothing more than financial commodities, the reason one spends money to buy a purebred or a particular mix (the ubiquitous "A-Poo" dogs—Cockapoo, Pekeapoo, Pomapoo, and so on), is so one will be able to predict how the dog will look and act. Sometimes one buys a particular breed for status; as in, "I have the only Anatolian Bear Dog in the state," or for function; if one hunts, farms, or wants some help chasing gazelles. The function of the dog is not to produce revenue; it is to be a guardian, companion, rat-chaser, foot-warmer, bird-fetcher, or whatever. Furthermore, most breeders' dreams of financial empire come crashing down when the realities hit: unexpected vet bills, possible loss of puppies and/or mother, half a dozen unsold adolescent puppies racing around, destroying the house and eating their heads off, and frantic attempts to find homes for them, even if the homes are not very good ones. Professional breeders can show you the statistics which prove that breeding dogs is a lousy way to make money.

"Poopsie needs to have a litter to be fulfilled."

That comes from the same line of thought that insists that every woman must have a child to be fulfilled (whatever "fulfilled" means). You must not put human needs and values onto your dog. I promise you your dog has no

Fig. 17-2. *You could be stuck with many pups getting older and eating you out of house and home. Photo by Brenda Bartels.*

fantasies about the joys of motherhood, and many do not appreciate it when it is forced upon them. Not all bitches are naturally good mothers. Poopsie would be just as happy never having to share her life with anyone but you.

"But Ralph is a male, and males need sex."

In the dog, sex is a reflexive behavior, like defecation (although more complex). There is no romance involved, no thoughts of conquest, no macho image. Again, beware of putting human needs and values onto your dog. By the way, neutered males have a much lower incidence of prostate problems as they age.

"I want to breed Poopsie so my children will understand the miracle of new life" (read: sex).

There are two responses I always make to this statement. The first is that if you want the children to understand the miracle of life, they must also understand the miracle of death. Immediately after they see the puppies born, take them to the local animal shelter so they can see dogs being killed. In this way, they will learn that reproduction goes hand in hand with responsibility. The second response was made by a professional breeder in answer to a woman who stated the above reason for wanting to breed her female to the breeder's champion male. "Why don't you", suggested the breeder, "let your children watch you and your husband, and leave the poor dog in peace?"

"I heard all females should have one litter before they are spayed."
This is an old wive's tale that has no basis in fact. The truth is that there is no medical reason why a bitch should have a litter. In fact, bitches spayed before their first heat cycle have a lower incidence of breast cancer.

"I don't want to neuter my dog because it will change his/her personality."
There is some truth to this assertion, but people fail to understand that the change, if any, is always for the better. I have seen neutering calm an aggressive dog and relax a shy dog. Occasionally, I have seen dramatic effects in reversal of these behaviors. I have never seen it have a negative effect on any dog.

"Neutered dogs get fat and lazy."
Neutered dogs get fat for the same reason un-neutered dogs get fat: their owners give them too much food and too little exercise. In some dogs, there are metabolic changes after neutering which result in the dog's needing less food to maintain its ideal weight. If you neuter your dog, keep an eye on his or her weight (see p. 147) for several months following surgery. If the dog is plumping up, cut his food back a little at a time until you find the correct amount to feed. I have never known neutering to affect a dog's energy level. Many top obedience contenders are neutered, as are many dogs working in field activities (hunting and lure coursing). Neutering does not affect a dog's ability to guard you and your home.

BEFORE YOU BREED

If you can't answer "yes" to *all* of these questions, think again about why you want to breed.

<table>
<tr><td></td><td>**Yes**</td><td>**No**</td></tr>
<tr><td>1. My dog has a sound temperament. He or she is friendly, confident, curious and trustworthy (*no* excuses accepted!).</td><td>☐</td><td>☐</td></tr>
<tr><td>2. My dog is in good health, free of parasites.</td><td>☐</td><td>☐</td></tr>
<tr><td>3. My dog's hips have been x-rayed and pronounced free of dysplasia by a qualified veterinary radiologist.</td><td>☐</td><td>☐</td></tr>
<tr><td>4. My dog's eyes have been checked and cleared by a veterinary ophthalmologist.</td><td>☐</td><td>☐</td></tr>
<tr><td>5. My dog is free of seizures.</td><td>☐</td><td>☐</td></tr>
<tr><td>6. If my dog is a purebred, it is registered with the AKC or UKC and is a good specimen of its breed (check with a professional breeder).</td><td>☐</td><td>☐</td></tr>
<tr><td>7. If my dog is a mixed-breed it is an attractive, sound-looking animal.</td><td>☐</td><td>☐</td></tr>
<tr><td>8. I am aware of other diseases and hereditary conditions common to the breed (or mix of breeds) that I own, and my dog has been tested and found medically clear of these diseases and hereditary conditions.</td><td>☐</td><td>☐</td></tr>
<tr><td>9. I am prepared to spend whatever money is necessary for pre-natal care, veterinary expenses for mother and puppies, and stud fees.</td><td>☐</td><td>☐</td></tr>
<tr><td>10. I am prepared to keep all of the puppies for as long as it takes to find good, loving homes for them. If I own a large breed, I have adequate space to raise numerous growing puppies.</td><td>☐</td><td>☐</td></tr>
<tr><td>11. I am willing to investigate potential puppy-buyers to be sure all family members want the puppy and that they understand how to care for the puppy or are willing to learn.</td><td>☐</td><td>☐</td></tr>
<tr><td>12. I am prepared to take back any puppies that do not work out in their original homes, and keep them until I can place them in new homes.</td><td>☐</td><td>☐</td></tr>
</table>

"My female is very shy. I want her to have a litter of puppies so she will become more outgoing. It worked with her mother."

The above was actually said to me by a woman in one of my obedience classes. I explained to her that temperament was at least partly hereditary, as she might have observed, and that having a litter might settle her female, but so would spaying. Furthermore, if they were all going to have shy temperaments, what was the point of perpetuating the problem? And what about the shy males that couldn't have that magic litter? The bitch was spayed the next week and eventually settled into an acceptable pet. Neutering sometimes eliminates shy behavior. It frequently eliminates or diminishes aggressive behavior. Not only does neutering tend to calm both the shy and the aggressive dog, but it also seems to stabilize the dog's health. I have had several dogs who had chronic gastric problems (vomiting, diarrhea, refusal to eat). In all cases, the gastric problems disappeared within three months after the animal was neutered. I have no scientific basis for making this statement; it is merely the result of many years of observing dogs. Similarly, neutering frequently appears to "cure" poor eaters. I am not referring to the spoiled dog that has been given so many treats and table scraps he is no longer willing to eat dog food. I am talking about the dog who refuses to eat even canned or soft-moist dog food—no matter how palatable. I have had several non-eaters, and within a short time following neutering, they became eager eaters. A normal interest in food is important, both to the dog's general health and to a training program largely based on food rewards.

Some Final Thoughts

The dog that lives outside is not actually a part of your life and you are missing the opportunity to allow the dog to enhance it. Yes, it takes some time and effort to integrate an outside dog into your home life, but it is worth it, in terms of the depth of the relationship you will build with him. The training really doesn't take very long, and the time you must invest to teach the dog to behave in the house is well spent. Even if you and the dog both prefer that he sleep outside, bring him in in the morning when you are getting ready for work or in the evening when you are relaxing. Let him show you his personality and his own peculiar charm. Show him yours. Enjoy each other, don't isolate yourselves.

I hope this book has started you thinking about how you relate to your dog and to any other creatures for whom you have accepted responsibility. The techniques you have learned represent one way to teach and relate to your dog. If you can invent other humane ways to accomplish the same end, by all means do so. Dog training can be as creative as anything else you do. Use this opportunity to explore the strengths and limitations of both the dog's character and your own. Having a positive and loving relationship with your dog is one of the few certainties in this busy, confusing world you both inhabit.

BIBLIOGRAPHY

OBEDIENCE TRAINING BOOKS

If you'd like to pursue further training, here are a number of books I recommend.

Bauman, Diane. *Beyond Basic Dog Training*, Howell, N.Y., 1986.
Diane is one of the top competition trainers in the country today. She is creative, innovative and humorous. This book will take you and your dog through all levels of competitive training.

Burnham, Patricia Gail. *Play Training Your Dog*. St. Martin's Press, N.Y. 1980.
One of my favorite training books. Takes you through all levels of training for obedience competition. Easy to read, funny and humane.

Handler, Barbara. *Best Foot Forward, The Complete Guide to Obedience Handling*, Alpine Publications, Loveland, CO, 1984.
If you plan to compete in an obedience trial with your dog, this book tells you what you can and can't do.

Parris, Max. *Training to the Maximum*, Printing Galore, Chattanooga, TN, 1985.
The first book to take the trainer and dog all the way through the first level of obedience competition detailing the methodical use of positive reward and correction. Very clear and easy to follow.

Pearsall, Margaret E. *The Pearsall Guide to Successful Dog Training*, Howell, N.Y., 1973.
This book was one of the first to use positive methods rather than pain avoidance training. The Pearsalls, Milo and Margaret, were active in the world of obedience as trainers and judges for many years. They were also among the first to teach practical puppy training. Takes you through all levels of obedience training.

Volhard, Joachim & Fisher, Gail. *Training Your Dog-The Step by Step Manual*, Howell, N.Y., 1983.
Another very detailed outline of first level training, mostly using positive reward.

TRICK TRAINING

Berwick, Ray. *How to Train Your Pet Like a Television Star,* Armstrong, Los Angeles, 1977.
This and the two books that follow are well-illustrated, clearly written books about a fun subject.

Haggerty, Capt. Arthur and Benjamin, Carol Lea. *Dog Tricks,* Doubleday, Garden City, N.Y., 1978.

Mr. Lucky. *Mr. Lucky's Trick Dog Training,* Denlingers, Fairfax, VA, 1987.

PET-FACILITATED THERAPY

Beck, Allen and Katcher, Aaron, *Between Pets and People: The Importance of Animal Companionship,* Putnam, N.Y., 1983.
This is a readable book about human-animal bonding and ways pet-facilitated therapy is used.

White, Betty. *Pet Love: How Pets Take Care of Us,* Pinnacle Books N.Y., 1985.
A charming book by the well-known actress and animal lover. Easy to read and not at all technical.

BEHAVIORAL PROBLEMS

Benjamin, Carol Lea. *Dog Problems,* Doubleday, Garden City, N.Y., 1981.
An excellent book covering everything from barking to digging to biting. Written clearly, with humor and compassion for dog and owner. My one complaint: she does not advocate neutering for aggressive dogs. I recently spoke to Job Michael Evans who gives seminars with Ms. Benjamin, and he said she now advocates neutering (along with training) in cases of aggression.

The Monks of New Skete. *How To Be Your Dog's Best Friend,* Little, Brown, Boston, MA, 1978.
This is a terrific book on establishing a positive relationship with your dog. It was one of the first books for the general public that dealt with dominance and alpha issues, as well as puppy rearing, how to read a pedigree, etc. Unfortunately, the Brothers recommend pain avoidance training using choke collars. If you just ignore the training section, this is an excellent book.

PUPPY TRAINING

Neill, David and Rutherford, Clarice. *How to Raise a Puppy You Can Live With.* Alpine Publications, Loveland, CO, 1981.
> A complete, well-written guide to choosing and raising a sane, well-adjusted dog. I recommend it highly.

DOG PSYCHOLOGY

Fox, Michael, D.V.M. *Understanding Your Dog*, Bantam, N.Y., 1977.
> This book is written for the general public, and aside from an unfortunate prejudice against purebred dogs, presents a wealth of knowledge on the mental and emotional development of the dog.

Pfaffenberger, Clarence, *The New Knowledge of Dog Behavior.* Howell Book House, N.Y., 1963.
> The author developed the information in this book by observation and experimentation at one of the schools that train guide dogs for the blind. It was the first book on dog behavior written for the public, rather than for other professionals.

Pryor, Karen. *Don't Shoot the Dog*, Bantam Books, N.Y., 1984.
> This is a moderately technical book about the learning process, focusing on shaping behavior through positive reinforcement. Don't be put off by having to learn a few technical psychological terms. This is an excellent book with implications for human behavior. It is readable and informative.

HEALTH PROBLEMS

Gerstenfeld, Sheldon, D.V.M. *Taking Care of Your Dog*, Addison Wesley, Reading, MA, 1979.
> An excellent book for the pet owner. Gives physical signs of all common illnesses and indicates whether home remedies or professional care is needed. Clearly written and well organized.

Vine, Louis L., D.V.M. *Your Dog, His Health and Happiness*, Arco, N.Y., 1971.
> A standard text for pet owners. Not as up to date as I would like, especially regarding behavior problems, but a good reference book.

GROOMING

Kohl, Sam and Goldstein, Catherine, *The All Breed Dog Grooming Guide*, Arco, N.Y., 1975.

Stone, Ben and Pearl. *The Stone Guide to Dog Grooming for All Breeds*, Howell, N.Y., 1982.
> This is a well illustrated, clearly written volume that addresses the grooming needs of all purebred dogs recognized by the AKC. It gives both show and pet grooming instructions. If you have a mixed breed, you might look through this book until you find the purebred that looks most like your dog and then groom accordingly.

CHOOSING A DOG

AKC, *The Complete Dog Book*, Howell, N.Y., 1983.
> Published and updated frequently, this book contains the written descriptions of the ideal specimen of each breed recognized by the AKC.

Caras, Roger. *The Roger Caras Dog Book: A Guide to Purebred Dogs*, Holt, Rinehart, N.Y., 1980.
> A charming and informative description of each breed. Well-written but not altogether an accurate assessment.

INDEX

A special thanks to the people and dogs who appeared in the photographs:

Readers who would like to learn more about their dog and its care are referred to the following Alpine titles:

How to Raise a Puppy You Can Live With
Rutherford & Neil $6.98
The puppy owner's "Dr. Spock." A must for every new puppy owner; takes the puppy from birth to one year. How a pup's body and mind develop, puppy training, socialization, puppy testing, owner's responsibilities.
126 pgs., paper. ISBN 0-931866-09-X

What's Bugging Your Dog, A Guide to Canine Parasitology
Schneider $5.98
This book will help you help your veterinarian identify parasite problems, or save you many times its cost by learning to identify parasites yourself with the aid of a student's microscope.
60 pgs., paper. ISBN 0-931866-19-7

Alpine Publications • 214 19th St. S.E. • Loveland, CO 80537